EXPERIENCING CHRISTMAS

Experiencing Christmas:
Christ in the Sights and Sounds of Advent

Experiencing Christmas
978-1-7910-2927-2
978-1-7910-2928-9 *eBook*

Experiencing Christmas: Leader Guide
978-1-7910-2929-6
978-1-7910-2930-2 *eBook*

Experiencing Christmas: DVD
978-1-7910-2931-9

**Download a FREE children's leader guide
and youth study at
abingdonpress.com/experiencingchristmas.**

Also by Matt Rawle

The Faith of a Mockingbird
The Redemption of Scrooge
What Makes a Hero?
The Gift of the Nutcracker
The Grace of Les Miserables
The Heart that Grew Three Sizes
Jesus Revealed

For more information, visit MattRawle.com.

MATT RAWLE

EXPERIENCING CHRISTMAS

CHRIST IN THE SIGHTS AND SOUNDS OF ADVENT

Abingdon Press | Nashville

Experiencing Christmas
Christ in the Sights and Sounds of Advent

Library of Congress Control Number: 2023936272

978-1-7910-2927-2

MANUFACTURED IN THE UNITED STATES OF AMERICA

CONTENTS

INTRODUCTION
EXPERIENCING CHRISTMAS

Stop. For a moment pay attention to what you're hearing. Are you the kind of person who reads when it's quiet, with no outside distractions? Maybe you can only read when it's busy and loud, the hustle and bustle of life creating a white noise allowing you to concentrate. Where are you reading? What do you see? Obviously, the words on this page are calling for your attention, but what else do you see? Are you reading outside in the sunlight? Maybe you're in an office under the fluorescents? Are you reading off a screen, or is lamplight dancing off the page? Do you snack while you read? I certainly do. I'm not too ashamed to say that I almost always have a can of almonds or a pack of gum at the ready when I know I'll be reading for a while. Maybe you read under the warmth of a blanket or outside in the nippy air. Do you lick your fingers and turn the page, or simply swipe from left to right to see what's next?

We don't make sense without our senses. Everything we understand, everything we communicate, and everything we imagine is filtered through what we can see, hear, touch, smell, and taste. Have you ever tried sitting and thinking about nothing, being aware enough to know that you aren't paying attention to what you see or smell or feel? I've never been able to achieve that kind of mindfulness. I've heard that this kind of meditation can make you feel closer to God, and although I'm sure this is true, the Christmas story encourages the opposite.

Christmas is the celebration that God now has senses. God put on flesh in the person of Jesus to experience and redeem humanity in a unique and radical way. Instead of us burning offerings so our prayers may rise to the heavens, God has come down to us. God has come near to smell the sweetness of our incense and the mustiness of poverty. As we hunger and thirst for righteousness, God now knows what it's like to hunger and thirst after the daily search for a meal. Through the Incarnation, God-in-flesh, God has made the chasm between heaven and earth very small indeed.

We seem to acknowledge this intuitively as we prepare for Christmas. Advent is a season set apart like no other. Everything seems different at the end of the year. We put lights on our houses to dispel the growing darkness, Christmas music floods local radio stations, apple cider and cranberry sauce are once again on the menu, and wrapping paper and tape are always at the ready. Things just look, smell, and taste different during the Advent and Christmas season. It's as if creation itself is groaning and searching for God's intervention. Everything seems different at the end of the year because everything was different when Jesus breathed his first breath in Bethlehem. That's what we'll explore together in this book. In each chapter, we'll consider one of our senses and its unique encounters during Advent—things we see, hear, taste, and touch. We'll discover how those senses become signs for us, pointing to the Incarnation when God took on human flesh and experienced the world as we do.

What does it mean for God to have senses, and what does it have to do with us? Let's begin with sight. After all, most of our brain power is dedicated to sight. My wife and I both wear glasses, but our vision is quite different. She's effectively blind without her glasses, and she calls my prescription a windshield because there's hardly any change at all. I wonder if Jesus would have worn glasses. Should we assume that Jesus's vision was perfect? Is needing a prescription a sin? Certainly not, but do we feel uncomfortable thinking that Jesus's eyesight might have needed correcting? It may seem a silly thing, but Jesus had two eyes just like us. If something was outside the periphery, Jesus didn't see it. But in other ways, Jesus saw more than we see. When a woman bathed Jesus's feet with her tears, he asked his host, "Do you see this woman?" (Luke 7:44). Simon the Pharisee could only see her sin. How often do our eyes fall short of this divine compassion? The Christmas story reminds us that God now sees both what we see and what we fail to see.

Several years ago, a friend was gracious enough to give me a ride to a meeting. His car radio was playing a talk show, and, hoping to change the station, I asked him what his favorite kind of music was. He said that he didn't have one. I was at a loss for words. To me, not having a favorite kind of music is like saying that you only drink clam juice. I'm sure it's possible, but what a sad way to journey through life. Maybe you don't listen to music, and this sounds perfectly normal. I was a music major in college, and I can't imagine what life would be like without music. My life has a constant soundtrack playing in my headphones. But I wonder if Jesus might have been more like my friend than I care to admit. Did Jesus have a favorite kind of music? Maybe that question doesn't even make sense in the ancient world. Did people have to speak up when talking to Jesus, or was there a holiness about him that prompted hushed whispers? I don't mind hearing people chew, but some find the sound stomach-churning. Did Jesus ever find certain sounds annoying? Maybe cries for healing, the sound of desperation and lament, were as unpalatable to Jesus's ears as nails scraped across a chalkboard. Maybe those sounds called attention to injustice or a need for Jesus to act, to teach, restore, heal.

What kind of food do you think Jesus preferred? Did Jesus ever know the calming scent of lavender? Did Jesus find wool itchy? These are silly questions, but they point to a profound truth. God put on flesh and all that comes with it—growing pains, thirsting after a long day's journey, the joy of an early morning stretch, tired feet, sunburned skin, and even the suffering of crucifixion. God entered into God's own creation so that the line between heaven and earth might be thin.

During Christmas, our senses are saturated with music, visuals, food, textures, and holiday scents—of course they are. Christmas celebrates that God now has senses—eyes to see suffering and ears to hear lament, knowing the saltiness of tears and the desire for compassionate touch. God doesn't experience humanity and simply let it be. God enters into our story so that our story might be redeemed. "This will be a sign to you," the angel announces to the shepherds. They didn't see fire on the mountain or parted waters. They didn't see wheels upon wheels and dry bones dancing. There were no burning altars or gale-force winds. They saw a baby wrapped snugly, lying in a manger. They saw that God had emptied the divine to reveal a vulnerable love to a mother and a man, relying on humanity to save humanity. As we adorn our houses with lights and fill our sanctuaries with Christmas songs, bring out the figgy pudding and wrap the gifts for Christmas morning, may all of our senses and all that we are, celebrate the night God put on flesh and dwelt among us!

CHAPTER ONE

DO YOU SEE WHAT I SEE?

CHAPTER ONE

DO YOU SEE
WHAT I SEE?

*In those days Caesar Augustus declared that every-
one throughout the empire should be enrolled in
the tax lists.*

(Luke 2:1)

What is your fondest Advent or Christmas memory? Does
this memory have something to do with decorating a tree full of
ornaments, each holding a memory of its own? Maybe it doesn't
quite feel like Christmas until the choir sings *The Messiah* or that

special song that only your congregation sings year after year. Sometimes there's a special dish a loved one whips up for the family gathering that you only have around the holidays. Maybe it's the smell of gingerbread or even wrapping paper and tape that immediately transports you to your childhood home on the night before Christmas. Or maybe it's the warmth of a mug of cocoa in your hand, or the brush of your fingers against pine needles?

These moments, taken separately or together as a season of senses, are what it means to experience Christmas. The sights, sounds, smells, and tastes are just different during the holidays. Talking about resurrection and singing "Christ the Lord Is Risen Today" feels fine almost any time of year, but sing "Silent Night" in July, or don't sing "Silent Night" on December 24th, and you just might start a riot. It's not our liturgical senses that are offended. Our actual senses are. Having a Christmas tree in your living room in March feels about as sensical as eating soup in the summer or wearing shorts to a snowball fight. Christmas is so tied to our collective memory because it is so intimately connected to our senses. These holiday experiences are hard to forget, for good or ill.

Luke's Nativity story begins with the words, "In those days Caesar Augustus declared that everyone throughout the empire should be enrolled in the tax lists." *In those days* there was a proclamation from the one who held the most power. That declaration went out to the corners of the Roman Empire. Luke's story begins in the past, but how far back in the past? Just how far back is the period in question, "in those days"?

4

In the beginning, when God began creating the heavens and the earth, God said, "Let there be light." In *those* days the one who held all power spoke, and that declaration *shaped* the four corners of the world. As far as introductions go, John's Gospel usually gets top billing as the narrative that calls the reader to remember creation. John's "In the beginning was the Word," certainly tunes our ears to remember "In the beginning God created the heaven and the earth" (Genesis 1:1 KJV); but by bringing to mind that the one who holds the power proclaims a word that is to spread throughout the world, Luke's Gospel, in its own way, is also calling us to remember the beginning.

God said, "Let there be light: and there was light. And God saw the light, that it was good" (Genesis 1:3-4 KJV). God spoke, and then saw. God saw the light and saw that it was good. God then separated the waters from the waters and saw that it was good. God made the dry land and saw that it was good. The sun, moon, and stars, the vegetation, the creeping things, and then humanity...and saw that it was good. The creation unfolds through the repetition of those two actions: "God said..." and "God saw..." I can almost imagine that God's eyes were closed in that first utterance of "let there be," and maybe there really wasn't much to see anyway. With eyes closed God speaks, and then when God's voice ceases to reverberate through the cosmos, God opens divine eyes and sees that the light is good.

When we are born, we cry with eyes closed, then we open our eyes to look up at the one who gave us birth. For a moment, everything is good. At our beginning we remember *the* beginning. God spoke and then saw. We speak and then see. I wonder if God

5

offers this reminder of creation at our creation just to say that we are already loved from the beginning of our story.

God spoke and then saw, though God saw creation from the perspective of creator. Try as we might, we cannot comprehend the chasm between creator and creation. We cannot perceive what it means for anything to exist outside of creation. God knows we can't. This is what Christmas is about. God entered into creation with eyes of God's own, so that we might see God's love clearly. Christmas is the beginning of heaven and earth becoming one, where the dividing line between Creator and Creation, and the dividing line between you and me, is dissolved. When time was "full," God began to experience humanity like never before.

What does it mean for God now to have eyes? Did God in Jesus have perfect vision? We ponder, "Do you see what I see," knowing now that God just might ask us the same question.

A DISTANT GLOW

When you see a box of Christmas lights, what do you see? Do you see the potential for an amazing display, artfully adorning your home signifying the changing of the season from Thanksgiving to Advent and Christmas? Maybe these small filaments wrapped in plastic represent a winter wonderland or the first attempt at "lawn of the year." Maybe this role of wire and bulbs will soon be an illuminated scene depicting Christ's birth. Or do you see what I see: a fifty-foot ladder, clips that don't adhere to your roof, an afternoon of cursing the day you were born, and second-guessing your life choices? We may be looking at the same box of Christmas lights,

We ponder, "Do you see what I see," knowing now that God just might ask us the same question.

but what we see might be two very different things. What we can agree on is that Christmas just isn't Christmas without light.

Lights are one of the first signs that Christmas is near. Maybe more accurately, a lack of light begins to signal the changing season. At least for those of us north of the equator, the days begin to grow short. You start prepping for family dinner and by the time you set the table, the sun has set. For many, these short days offer an anxious anticipation for the next sunrise. There's almost a gnawing sensation when you know the day isn't over but the sun set hours ago. For others the darkness is no problem. The early evenings mean more time for campfires, more time to enjoy the lights around the neighborhood homes and businesses. Do you see what I see after the sun sets? Are you filled with anxiety? Do you experience excitement? (Maybe you see what I see . . . bedtime. I know it's only 8:00, but it's been dark for hours. Why spoil an opportunity for sleep?) Whether you experience anxiety or you are filled with excitement, we all tend to land in the same place. We all seem to agree that when it gets dark, we need more light. Either the light brings peace to the anxious heart or light offers beauty to those looking for some Christmas cheer. The light signals to us that something is different.

There are other visual signs too. We notice the change often when my family comes home from Thanksgiving. We typically spend a week galivanting across South Louisiana, seeing friends and family over the course of several Thanksgiving meals. When we leave our North Louisiana neighborhood, the houses appear normal, but when we come back everything looks different. There are reindeer in lawns, wreaths on streetlights, pop-up Christmas tree stands, inflatable Santas, and Salvation Army kettles in front of grocery stores. You don't have to be a Christian or a person of any faith tradition to recognize that change is in the air. You can see it with your own eyes.

Advent is a season of anticipation. "This is a sign for you," the angels tell the shepherds as they were "guarding their sheep at night." This is something you need to see. This is something to look for. When you see infants pulling up on the edge of the coffee table, you know they are soon to walk. When the fuel light illuminates on your car's dashboard, you know you need to get to a gas station. The inverted yield curve usually means a recession is ahead. We see these signs and anticipate what comes next. We almost seem hardwired for anticipation, to recognize that we live in a world of cause and effect. The relationship between what we see and how we respond is basic to our human condition. Sight is a powerful sense. More than 50 percent of our brain's cortex, the outer layer of our brain, is dedicated to sight.[1]

Seeing something in the distance, recognizing what it is, and responding correctly can be a life-or-death situation. A ship on the horizon can be friend or foe. The subtle movement in the bushes might be a bunny or a bear. Can I tell how far the oncoming headlights are before making this left-hand turn? Life is having the "capacity for anticipation," as John F. Haught puts it in his fantastic book *God After Einstein*. Anticipation is what separates us from God's magnificent work in the beginning of creation.[2] The light, seas, stars, and dry land cannot anticipate. They can offer signs of anticipation like a changing tide, a weathered rock, and a star that guides wise men from the east to find the new Messiah, but they in and of themselves do not anticipate. The arrival of life, for which the universe had to wait, gives a surprising, dramatic intelligibility for the three great immensities of time, space, and complexity. Only living creatures can anticipate, that is, see a sign and expect what will come next.

Sometimes I like to ponder just how long a "day" is meant to be during the Genesis 1 Creation account. The beautiful rhythm of light, water, and land, then creeping and swarming things, and animals, along with humanity, represents a story that is much grander than maybe we imagine. "Let there be light" may have been an utterance spoken an unfathomably long time ago. On our timeline, this light began to emerge over 13 billion years ago. Maybe the poet was on to something when he wrote: "In [God's] perspective a thousand years are like yesterday past" (Psalm 90:4). The data of both narrative and nature reveals that our participation in God's history constitutes just a sliver of time. How long did the universe have to wait until the universe could look back at itself? It took quite a long time—13.6 billion years— to anticipate a first look.

Anticipation can heighten the senses, inspiring either fight or flight. It usually begins with our feet. Either we anticipate standing our ground with feet planted firm, or our legs engage to get us away as quickly as we can. Thinking about feet and anticipation, this past summer I was reminded of a third category. There is fight, there is flight, and there is utter paralysis. I have a love-hate relationship with water. I love looking at water. I love the sound of the waves crashing against the shoreline. Seeing the vastness of the ocean inspires thoughts of the immensity of God's grace, but

I hate being in the water. Being on top of the water in a boat or on a pier is absolutely fine, but being in the water causes a cascade of problems for me. First, as a young child I constantly had ear infections during the summer, so eventually if I wanted to swim I had to wear ear plugs and a swim cap. I also wasn't the slimmest of children. Being the chubby child having to wear a swim cap at parties makes for very long grade-school summers. Needless to say, I just didn't enjoy pool parties, and therefore I didn't spend much time at the pool. Secondly, I must have seen *Jaws* at much-too-young an age. If I ever did find myself in the deep end where my feet couldn't touch, all I could think about was how big the shark lurking just under the waves ready to eat me whole was.

This past summer I decided to give it another go. I swam out past the breaking waves and decided to swim past where my feet couldn't touch the sea floor. Then it happened. My body became still and unmoving, like I was playing a game of freeze tag. As soon as my feet couldn't ground me, I almost couldn't move. As soon as my head went under, thankfully flight kicked in and I swam as hard as I could to get back to shallow water. It's embarrassing, and I'm sure I'll tackle this fear at some point along my journey, but I didn't conquer it that day. In this case, anticipation led to anxiety. Do you see what I see when you see the ocean waves? Do you see a playground for surfing, fishing, and fun, or do you see something that must be avoided at all costs?

At the beginning of the Advent season, we dive into the prophetic poetry of the Hebrew Scriptures that our faith tradition has taught are signs for the coming Messiah. Jeremiah writes,

The time is coming, declares the LORD, when I will fulfill my gracious promise with the people of Israel and Judah. In those days and at that time, I will raise up a righteous branch from David's line, who will do what is just and right in the land. In those days, Judah will be saved and Jerusalem will live in safety. And this is what he will be called: The LORD Is Our Righteousness.

(Jeremiah 33:14-16)

I imagine Jeremiah writing his poetry in the evening illuminated by firelight, except Jeremiah isn't sitting near the hearth. He sees Jerusalem burning in the distance. Jeremiah, who was called to be a prophet in 625 BC, lived during the time of Judah's last kings. Sometimes called "The Weeping Prophet," Jeremiah's words were heavy, full of lament and warning. He was a "soul in pain," who "screamed, wept, moaned, and was left with a terror in his soul."[3]

On the one hand, the Lord proclaimed through Jeremiah, "The LORD's fierce anger won't turn back / until God's purposes are entirely accomplished. / In the days to come, / you will understand what this means." (Jeremiah 30:24). On the other hand, at times Jeremiah struggled with the harshness of his people's rejection of God—

I thought, I'll forget him;
I'll no longer speak in his name.
But there's an intense fire in my heart,
trapped in my bones.

12

I'm drained trying to contain it;
I'm unable to do it.
(Jeremiah 20:9)

Jeremiah lived with a polarity of despair and hope, dancing between terror and grace, offering both warning and pardon to a people seemingly deaf to both. What better character to shift our gaze, to help us see something else within that distant glow? The fire is destructive, but it also symbolizes God's new, righteous branch rising from the smoldering rubble. As Walter Brueggemann writes:

> What a commission it is to express a future that none think imaginable! Of course this cannot be done by inventing new symbols, for that is wishful thinking. Rather, it means to move back into the deepest memories of this community and activate those very symbols that have always been the basis for contradicting the regnant consciousness. Therefore the symbols of hope...must be those that have been known concretely in this particular history...to those deep symbols, they will discern that hope is not a late, tacked-on hypothesis to serve a crisis but rather the primal dimension of every memory of this community...[which] begins in God's promissory address to the darkness of chaos.[4]

There's more to Advent than waiting in anticipation. There is hope. If it were only anticipation Jeremiah might anticipate an everlasting Babylonian Empire as they sack the Jerusalem Temple. He would anticipate a people destroyed and a God forgotten. Yet

13

There's more to Advent than waiting in anticipation. There is hope.

the prophet articulates hope that even in the fire, God is doing something wonderful. When the days grow increasingly short in the autumn, we anticipate that nights will lengthen. Yet we hope that light will dispel the darkness. What kind of light do we envision? What kind of light are we expecting, and what might it mean? A devastating fire certainly illuminates the night sky, but at what cost? Jeremiah is asking, "Do you see what I see?"

THE HOLLY AND THE IVY

What are those visual markers of the season that represent something new is about to happen? The symbols we see during Advent are important. The familiar symbols of the Christmas tree, the holly and the ivy, the wreath, and the candles need little explanation in our popular imagination, and yet they represent a hope that can be difficult to see without prophetic fervor.

With little exception, every Advent in my congregation begins with a "Hanging of the Greens" worship experience independent of our Sunday morning worship. The first Sunday in Advent the table is relatively bare, the decorations sparse. The Scripture reading and message for the day are deeply rooted in prophets like Jeremiah, offering a tension between tragedy and hope. It is the only worship experience of the year that is intended to feel "intertestamental." The Old Testament is remembered, but we aren't quite in the New Testament just yet. The pomp and majesty of Christ the King Sunday seems longer ago than last week, and it also doesn't feel quite right to jump into Advent. Not yet.

The service on this first Sunday morning of Advent is simple and stripped down as if there's not enough time for something as frivolous as decorations as we hold our breath between Malachi and Matthew. The prophet says,

> Look, I am sending Elijah the prophet to you,
>> before the great and terrifying day of the LORD
>> arrives.
> Turn the hearts of the parents to the children
>> and the hearts of the children to their parents.
>>> Otherwise, I will come and strike the land
>>> with a curse.
>
> *(Malachi 4:5-6)*

We wait, lingering on the prophet's words, giving ourselves space to anticipate and hope for the Gospel: "A record of the ancestors of Jesus Christ, son of David, son of Abraham" (Matthew 1:1). The morning service is meant to feel ambiguous, leaving you with unanswered questions searching for more definitive answers. This is more than a clever strategy to get the congregation to return for the evening "Hanging of the Greens" (though it is a great strategy to do just that!). The experience captures the anticipation of Advent. The service ends with the feeling of "and then…"

When the congregation returns in the evening, we finally hear the familiar tune of "O Come, O Come, Emmanuel," which heralds, in song, the familiar hope. Gathering in the evening outside of the normal worship order gives us permission to craft a different kind of experience. Using musical arrangements from bands like The Brilliance and Page CVXI signals that something different is around the corner. We decorate and light the Chrismon tree within the context of worshipful work and liturgical prayer. The children strand garlands around the sanctuary in a parade reminiscent of their palm-waving "Hosannas" the Sunday before Easter. We pray over the Advent wreath as we light the candle of hope. Lights, colorful fabric, poinsettias, and maybe a sweater or two signal that it's finally the time to prepare for the coming of the Lord.

These symbols of our faith—the tree, the wreath, the lights, and the holly and the ivy—all represent the "deep symbols" that not only root us in a shared, collective, and trusted (and maybe dangerously nostalgic) memory, but they are necessary symbols of hope. When we bless the chrismon tree we pray, "Holy Lord, we come with joy to celebrate the birth of your Son, / who rescued us from the darkness of sin / by making the cross a tree of life and light."[5] The tree isn't just adorned with lights and ornaments. It represents a future hope of salvation through the justifying grace of God in Christ. The prayer for the Advent Wreath details an expectation that light can conquer the "darkness of ignorance and sin."[6] When we light the candle of hope, we invite the congregation into a different future trajectory.

Do you see what I see when we bless, parade, and illuminate these symbols of our faith? The decorations represent more than the coming of a new season. In a very real sense, these symbols mark the crucial transition between anticipation and expectation. They are the bridge between seeing a distant fire and assuming a destructive finality and recognizing that the blaze is burning away the old so that the new can come into fruition. It is the difference between Jerusalem being destroyed and a "new shoot" sprouting.

Advent is not a season of anticipation. Anticipation is incomplete. Anticipation does not require hope. Advent is not a time for studying trends or waiting on markets or replicating programmatic calendars for a new ministry year. That is anticipation—responding to what is known, looking for what is likely. When we make room for hope, our anticipation becomes expectation: the mystery of faith, trading certainty for blessed surprise, exchanging the safety of rhythm for the risk of improvisation, letting go of our assumptions of finitude for the glory of abundant life. Jeremiah wasn't anticipating the destruction of Jerusalem. His prophecies were expecting a coming Messiah. Anticipation is assuming that exile is the end of the story. Expectation is the falling upward of grace. Do you see what I see in these symbols of our faith? They are the transition between anticipation and expectation, or as Psalm 30:5 puts it—

> *His anger lasts for only a second,*
> *but his favor lasts a lifetime.*
> *Weeping may stay all night,*
> *but by morning, joy!*

We anticipate the weeping lingering of the night, but we, through these Advent and Christmas symbols, expect the joy of morning.

FROM ANTICIPATION TO EXPECTATION

Chris Hemsworth, best known for his role of Thor in the Marvel Cinematic Universe, is also the narrator of a Disney Plus program titled, *Limitless with Chris Hemsworth. Limitless* explores the limits of the human body, offering "fascinating insights into how we can all unlock our body's superpowers to fight illness, perform better and even reverse the aging process."[7] Throughout the show, Hemsworth completes a series of extraordinary challenges to test these new scientific theories. Hemsworth's hosting offers a tragic irony. During the course of the series, Hemsworth had his DNA tested and discovered his genetic makeup includes two copies of the gene APOE4, one from his mother, the other from his father, which studies have linked to an increased risk of Alzheimer's disease. One in four people carry a single copy of the gene, but only 2 to 3 percent of the population have both, according to a 2021 study by the National Institutes of Health.[8] This makes him ten times more likely to develop Alzheimer's.

Knowing this information, you might anticipate suffering, sadness, and a feeling of defeat, which are all honest and appropriate emotions. Hemsworth said in a *Vanity Fair* article, "You don't know what tomorrow holds, so live it to its fullest. Whether or not [knowing about the disease] helps you live longer, it's about living better right now. Whatever you do right now to benefit your future self is having a huge benefit in your current self."[9] Finding out that he had a genetic predisposition for Alzheimer's wasn't what he was anticipating, but now he is expecting to live a full life every day.

The journey from anticipation to expectation hinges on hope. When your child comes home with less than perfect grades, you may anticipate difficulty in the future, but are you expecting to see a brilliant mind coming into fruition, struggling with the

The journey from anticipation to expectation hinges on hope.

current rules because they will be writing new ones for the rest of us? Maybe you've been told that this is the last year you will be with your current employer. I'm sure you're anticipating hardship and a difficult season, but are you expecting a new freedom and a new opportunity to jump into something truly life-giving? What are you anticipating about tomorrow? What are you expecting to happen? How do you know the difference? Anticipation is knowing how to catch a ball because of the way it is thrown. Expectation is looking for someone who wants to play catch. Anticipation is based on what is known. Expectation never is. How do you define the difference between anticipation and expectation in your story?

When we were having our first child, my wife devoured the book *What to Expect When You're Expecting.* In theory the book is a helpful guide for awareness during the confusing time of a first pregnancy. In practice the title should more appropriately be *What to Be Paranoid About When You're Expecting.* My wife, Christie, wanted to do everything perfectly: caloric intake with the best foods for brain development, aerobic exercise to build stamina, the perfect blend of supplements for peak immunity, and a host of other things. Of course, there's nothing wrong with any of this, though through subsequent pregnancies we've discovered just how resilient and amazing a mother's body is. Even when eating too much salmon or skipping the daily walk, all of our kids (despite the DNA they've inherited from their father) are wonderful. I know not every story ends well, and I grieve with those for whom even this paragraph brings to the surface difficult memories. What to expect when you're expecting? Expect that no two journeys are the same.

Without preparation, anticipation makes no sense. Anticipation is the fruit of previous knowledge, skill, and deduction, and its goal is an appropriate course of action for what is coming. Conversely, you can't prepare for expectation, at least not actively. The only way to "prepare" for expectation is through imagination. The hope found within expectation is the acceptance of unfettered possibility. You can prepare for the birth of a child, but you should expect that the child will be and do many things that surprise you, that you will never see coming.

The role of surprise and possibility applies to our spiritual journey. We can envision our spiritual walk as a story in three chapters. In the first chapter you build a "God box," into which you place all of your ideas, thoughts, and assumptions about God. This begins at an early age regardless of whether you were raised within a faith community. We all have ideas that there is an "other." That other must be bigger, better, faster, stronger than we.

It's easy to see how our first idea about God is that God simply is bigger, because early in our story, everything is bigger than we are. Chairs adults use to sit on are the very things on which we pull to stand up. You realize that there was something here before you were here, and so the "other" must be old, at least older than you. You have a hard time moving heavy things, but adults seem to struggle little, so the divine must be even stronger than grown-ups. God must be up in the sky somewhere because with your feet on the ground it seems an impossible place to be. It's no surprise that our first thoughts about God are that there is someone or something bigger, older, stronger, and full of the impossible.

These divine attributes are beautiful, and they serve us well. At some point these characteristics begin to change. The second chapter in this spiritual story begins when our thoughts about God change. Think about those first few math lessons from elementary school about subtraction. You're told at an early age that you can't subtract a bigger number from a smaller number. Then one day you're taught that you can. The only difference is that previously you weren't able to conceive of something like a negative number. At some point you may consider that God might not be bigger than everything. Maybe God doesn't have a body at all? Maybe it's not that God is stronger than anything, able to move mountains or barriers, but maybe God wants us to level the mountains and make the rough places plain (Isaiah 40:3-4) so that God can be seen clearly. Maybe God isn't older than we are, but God isn't bound by time in the same way. In this way, eternity is about being unbound rather than how long our experience of heaven may be. It's not that God lives up there and out there as much as we understand that God lives in each one of us.

The "God box" you've built will be taken apart as you grow in relationship with God and others. Eventually you'll build another box into which your new assumptions about God neatly fit. And then, you'll dismantle that one too. You will build up and tear down more than once, to the point when you think there are only two chapters in this story. The third chapter only begins when you realize that there is no need for a box because there is no box. No box can contain an inexhaustible, eternal, abundant, on-the-move God. This final step in this story, realizing that there is no box, is the place where expectation lives. You cannot prepare for expectation, except by opening your imagination to what you've never before seen.

Expectation changes what we see. Jeremiah sees a city burning to rubble and envisions righteousness, justice, and a new branch springing from ashes for all the world. We anticipate destruction, but Jeremiah looks with eyes of hope and offers the expectation of rebirth. How might expectation change your vision early in this Advent season? What are you anticipating that needs a touch of hope to become expectation?

Just before the Advent season we hosted a hymn sing at my local congregation. Much like John Wesley on his way to a society meeting on Aldersgate Street in 1738, I begrudgingly attended the hymn sing. As a vocal music major in undergrad, I love singing hymns; but it was late in November on a Wednesday evening, and with seemingly one hundred things still on my to-do list before Advent, I certainly didn't have time to sit and sing all the stanzas of "O For a Thousand Tongues to Sing." We invited participants to write down their favorite hymns and place them in a basket. Our lay leader would pull them out, name how many stanzas we would sing, and then cue the piano player. The event was scheduled for forty-five minutes to an hour, but after seeing something like sixty suggested hymns in the basket (at two to three stanzas per hymn), I realized that I should have brought a snack and a water bottle. This was going to take a while, and that didn't help my mood in the slightest.

But there was hope. Surely with sixty cards in the basket there had to be some duplicate suggestions, which would make the evening considerably shorter. There were ... only two. There were

Expectation changes
what we see. . . .
We anticipate
destruction, but
Jeremiah looks with
eyes of hope and offers
the expectation
of rebirth.

only two duplicate suggestions being "How Great Thou Art" and "Great Is Thy Faithfulness." I could almost hear God chuckling from heaven at my aggravation of how this hymn sing was infringing on my precious pastoral time. I was anticipating a long night and a sore throat. And then we sang "Blessed Assurance," and everything changed. As we started singing, I became tired and distracted so I stopped singing and started gazing about the room. I glanced over to see Ms. Jolene with her hymnal shut, hugging it against her heart. Her eyes were closed, and her head was tilted back as if she were singing to a divine audience of One. In that moment, nothing seemed more important to her. Seeing this holy moment unfold for her changed my narrow anticipation to an abundant expectation of what God was doing in her life and what God might be calling us to do in our faith community. Our hymn sing wasn't quite Jeremiah seeing a new shoot among the glowing embers of devastation, but it certainly changed me in my little world.

Anticipation becomes expectation in a moment of hopeful conviction. The Hebrew Scriptures fill us with a sense of anticipation for a child Messiah to be born.

> *Therefore, the Lord will give you a sign. The young woman is pregnant and is about to give birth to a son, and she will name him Immanuel.*
>
> *(Isaiah 7:14)*

> *A child is born to us, a son is given to us,*
> *and authority will be on his shoulders.*
> *He will be named*

Wonderful Counselor, Mighty God,
Eternal Father, Prince of Peace.
(Isaiah 9:6)

This is a sign for you: you will find a newborn baby
wrapped snugly and lying in a manger.
(Luke 2:12)

We are primed on Christmas Eve to anticipate seeing a baby, but do we expect to see salvation? When Jesus is presented to Simeon at the Temple eight days after his birth, Simeon says:

"Now, master, let your servant go in peace according
to your word,
    because my eyes have seen your salvation.
You prepared this salvation in the presence of all peoples.
It's a light for revelation to the Gentiles
    and a glory for your people Israel."
(Luke 2:29-32)

I mentioned that you can't prepare for expectation. That's true. You can't prepare for expectation in the same way you might for anticipation. It's not that the technique is different or that it takes special training. Yes, expectation lives in the place where "boxes" aren't, and our holy imagination needs to be big enough to "expect the unexpected." But you can't prepare for expectation because it is God who prepares for expectation. "My eyes have seen your salvation [that] you prepared...in the presence of all peoples." We can't prepare for the hopeful conviction the Holy Spirit offers, moving us from anticipation to expectation, but we can open our eyes and keep watch. We might anticipate having

27

to keep an eye on feckless sheep by moonlight, but the evening might end with the unbound expectation of what God will do through the sign of "a newborn baby wrapped snugly and lying in a manger" the angels in heaven announce.

CHRISTMAS LOOKS DIFFERENT

The first Sunday of Advent is a special Sunday because everything looks dramatically different than when we gathered last. The Christmas trees fill us with the anticipation of gifts, adorned with the symbols of our faith. But are we filled with the expectation of the cross, the expectation that there is more to the story for this tree, that one day it will be cut down and used for a symbol of death by an oppressive state? Are we expectant with hope that God will redeem it with an empty tomb? We anticipate a baby, but do we expect to see salvation? The Advent wreath leads us to anticipate peace, hope, love, and joy, but do we expect to *have* peace in our lifetime?

Experiencing Christmas is moving from anticipation into expectation. This time of year just looks different. Lights up on the rooftop, window displays of red and green and gold, trees in living rooms, SUVs with antlers and a red-nosed hood ornament (which I've seen surprisingly little of this year, and that's...OK). And it's not just the decorations that look different. There are more people serving with the poor, there are more people at local restaurants celebrating, there are more cars in the street and neighborhood because families are visiting. Things just look different this time of year because all of creation, with intent or accident, recognizes

We anticipate
a baby,
but do
we expect to
see salvation?

that when God put on flesh, everything changed. We look at the world and ask God, "Do you see what I see?" Do you see the hungry? Do you see the poor? Do you see those who are put down, messed up, ignored, or forgotten? Now, for the first time because God now has eyes to see, God answers with our same question: Do *you* see what I see? Do you see that soon the hungry will be filled, the poor will be blessed, the persecuted will leap for joy? I will walk among you, I will call you to follow, and together we will change the world.

QUESTIONS

1. What unique sights do you encounter during the weeks leading up to Christmas? How do these signify the coming birth of Jesus?

2. What is the difference between anticipation and expectation?

3. Imagine what Jesus saw when he lived. How much of it is the same as what you see today, and how much is different?

4. What do you think God sees when God looks at our world today?

5. How might expectation change your vision in this Advent season? What are you anticipating that needs a touch of hope?

CHAPTER TWO

DO YOU HEAR WHAT I HEAR?

CHAPTER TWO

Do You Hear
What I Hear?

*Sing to the L*ORD *a new song!*
Sing his praise from the ends of the earth!
You who sail the sea and all that fills it,
the coastlands and their residents.
(Isaiah 42:10)

Back in the spring of 1997, my dad and I went to "Spring Testing" at Louisiana State University, which was an opportunity for soon-to-be freshmen to test out of several core classes for many degree programs. On the last day, you had an opportunity to meet with a counselor to tour a specific area of the campus according to which major you would choose. The day before, we had breakfast at Louie's Café, a 24-hour diner that every LSU student knows. My dad, a chemist, leaned in over some hash browns and asked in what field I was thinking about majoring. As a child I wanted to be an astronomer or astrophysicist, always looking up at the night sky with awe and wonder. In middle school I wanted to own my own music publishing and producing conglomerate. Rawle Productions had its own logo and everything. In high school I considered being a pediatric ENT doctor. I had spent so many hours of my childhood in Dr. Owens's ENT office that I was certain I could skip half of med school. "So, what are you thinking, son?" my dad asked as the steam from the hash browns rose as incense to the heavens. "I think I want to be a music major," I said.

To say that there was an uncomfortable silence is like saying that the Beatles were an OK pop band. After blinking for what felt like an eternity, my dad asked a simple follow-up: "Are you sure?" I hesitated for just a beat, trying to read the importance of the moment, then I exhaled. "Yes, I'm sure." I said that I couldn't imagine a day without music. Music was the language I best understood, and it continues to be an inexhaustible source of expression, comfort, and joy.

Until my junior year of undergrad, it seemed like I ate, drank, and slept music. We had rehearsal every day and well into the night. Being a vocal music major also kept me out of a fair amount of trouble, I suppose. It's hard to sing the high note first thing in the morning if you're out late "rougarouin' around," as my grandmother used to say. But eventually singing began to feel more like a job than a joyful outlet for creativity. I started singing only for assignment completion. My voice wasn't achieving all that I had hoped. Coincidentally, I began feeling a call into ministry. I was on staff at University United Methodist Church in Baton Rouge. I found myself drawn to my second-floor youth director's office more than the third-floor music practice rooms. I changed my major from vocal performance to make room for a religious studies minor. I was moving away from a choir robe toward a preacher's robe.

Turning into my senior year when it was time to begin considering next steps, my dad asked me, "So, what are you thinking, Son?" Over the phone instead of hash browns this time, I replied, "I think I want to be a United Methodist pastor." To say that there was an uncomfortable silence is like saying Handel's *Messiah* is a fine piece of music. My dad replied, "Are you sure?" Feeling the moment "rhyme" with the conversation I had with my father four years prior, I took a breath and exhaled. "Yes." I said that I couldn't imagine a day without being in ministry.

Eventually I visited Duke Divinity School on an official visit. The time I spent on campus was exactly what I hoped it would be. I felt like God was calling me to move to Durham, North Carolina. But how could I be sure? I wrestled with the decision, wanting more certainty before committing to such a big step. I went into the Duke Chapel in the center of campus for a time of prayer. I thanked God for what seemed like a great opportunity, but I asked if this is where I needed to be. I sat in silence for fifteen minutes, and then I did what you aren't supposed to do. I asked for a sign. I asked God to offer me some kind of answer or acknowledgment—some way of indicating that Duke Divinity School was the right choice. It seemed to be a reasonable request. If God remained silent while I was in the chapel asking whether I should devote my life to serving, then that silence would have been deafening.

Nearly at that moment, the organ began to play. At first the sound took my breath away, as my face reflected an almost panicked surprise. Then, covering my face in my hands, I wept. God answered my prayer in the language I knew best. It was miraculous affirmation. Little did I know that the organ professor played in the chapel every day at 12:15, but isn't that how God works sometimes? An ordinary person praying a simple prayer, and a regular music professor doing what he loves to do. You put them together in the power of the Holy Spirit, and you have a life forever changed. The potential energy locked up in prayer explodes into the kinetic energy of twenty years of ministry, all ignited by a single, beautifully timed melody. Sight may be our most powerful sense, but the apostle Paul reminds us that "faith comes from listening" (Romans 10:17). He just might be right.

DID YOU HEAR THAT?

If "faith comes from listening," then Christmas must be the most faithful time of the year. As soon as you pack away your Halloween or fall festival costume, Christmas music seems to be on every radio station, Spotify header, and hobby store ambient shopping speaker. It's hard to know why there's more music this time of the year. It could be that music sparks a sense of nostalgia for more familiar times—times that weren't perfect or better, but expected, known, and comfortable. Or could it be that the excitement for gifts, end-of-the-year gatherings, and family coming home for an extended wintery stay produces music as a means of expression and celebration? I'd like to think that the peace, hope, love, and joy within the Advent liturgy demands more music for more worshipful gatherings, but I wonder if end-of-the-year marketing is the real inspiration for such a carol-inspired catalogue. Maybe there's more "jingle" to "Jingle Bells" than we care to admit.

Whatever the case, it seems impossible to imagine Christmas without music. If you have functioning ears, it's hard to imagine life without music. I'm sorry to have to tell you this because as soon as you hear it, you won't be able to unhear it. Next time you watch a movie on the big screen, notice how often a soundtrack is playing. I'm not just talking about the big, noticeable moments punctuated with orchestra, like "The Imperial March" when Darth Vader enters the scene. Notice the small things, like two characters talking about their next adventure or a panoramic shot setting up the next scene. Music is almost always underscoring the drama that we see on the screen. It almost seems silly to have so much music playing under the dialogue as if it's a departure from reality, but this is how we move through the world.

Disney executes this use of music as a backdrop extremely well in its theme parks, bringing movie magic into the real-life experience. When you're in Adventureland there is a constant underscoring of drums. Walking down Main Street you hear turn

It seems
impossible
to imagine
Christmas
without
music.

of the twentieth-century ragtime. Turning into Tomorrowland you hear electronic music suggesting that you've been whisked away into a future world. What we hear shapes our experiences and our emotional memories. Maybe this is why there is such a huge connection between Christmas and the nostalgia of "home."

We don't have orchestras walking around with us, but most of the time we can pinpoint the experience of emotion every moment of our lives. For example, right now what are you feeling? Are you excited that Christmas is just around the corner? Are you hurriedly reading because there aren't enough hours in the day? Maybe you're bored as your eyes move across the page. My guess is that you're feeling *something*, however mundane you think that emotion may be. In this moment you don't need an underscore to craft an emotion for you because you're living it; but watching a story unfold on the screen, we need the music's help to connect with the narrative.

Consider the soundtrack of the Christmas story. Imagine for a moment that you are one of the shepherds "guarding their flocks at night." What might occupy your ears? Ruminant animals, such as sheep, don't need much sleep, so maybe you listen for periodic bleating. Because there's little light, perhaps you listen for a change in the wind to know if there's incoming weather requiring shelter. Keeping watch at night has more to do with your ears than your eyes. I remember the first time I went camping. After sunset we settled in the tent with our flashlights, and eventually we had to turn out the lights and get some sleep. At first, I didn't hear anything out of the ordinary as I listened to the usual summer insects saying goodnight to each other in the whistling wind.

Every now and again there was an owl or something-or-other that broke the soothing monotony, but then I heard something I hadn't heard before. It was a new, unexpected sound. It wasn't loud or particularly ominous, but its unfamiliarity cut through the calming crickets with a frightening irregularity. Like a parent's eyes involuntarily popping open at the sound of a baby's cry, hearing something you don't expect to hear, especially while in the dark, is a jarring feeling.

Maybe for the shepherds the cracks and pops of a fire and the bleating of their flock were enough to keep them awake for what they assumed would be just another night. Then, I imagine, there was silence. The sheep make no sound. The wind stops. I assume there is a stillness that made the shepherds uneasy. For them I'm sure the silence was unsettling. Maybe this is the reason the angel who appeared in the night sky first announced, "Do not be afraid."

How do you imagine that first Christmas sounded? What story could be heard in addition to what our eyes might see? Maybe you imagine hearing "Joy to the World" when Jesus is born, or perhaps that is far too loud for a silent night. Maybe a more somber melody like "What Child Is This" is the best fit, but perhaps that doesn't adequately communicate the excitement we see from the shepherds who traveled with haste to find the Holy Family.

Because what we hear shapes our experiences, the sounds we hear every day help shape and share our identity. The New Orleans area is where I spent most of my childhood. Much like it's nearly impossible to experience Christmas without carols, it's hard to understand a city like New Orleans without the constant soundtrack of jazz, streetcars, neighborhood parades, and festivals. The Cajun, Creole, and Caribbean melting pot of a city creates a unique sound not found anywhere else. One of my favorite events in the city is the New Orleans Jazz and Heritage Festival. Every corner of the 145-acre outdoor venue is saturated with sound. From Cajun zydeco and modern jazz to the complicated history of Mardi Gras Indians and pop icons filling the *Billboard* charts, the two-weekend festival has just about everything. Interestingly, there seem to be just as many musical acts in the surrounding neighborhoods as there are within the fence of the fairgrounds. The neighborhoods around the fairgrounds are lined with local street musicians and walking brass bands. Music (as well as food, which we will talk about later) is the air that New Orleanians breathe.

I'm sure you have a soundtrack too. Maybe your community has its own musical identity, or your school or another organization has a song you sing together. You probably turn to certain kinds of music when you're in a given mood. Maybe you have a special song, or more than one, that's especially meaningful.

There are certain pieces of our soundtrack that most of us share. I bet if someone hums the first six notes of our National Anthem you will quite easily respond with, "By the dawn's early light." Or when the lights on a birthday cake are presented to a child after dinner and someone says, "Haaaaaaaappppy…" I imagine you know how to finish that sentence without any direction at all. On the largest scale, music reveals that we might share more in common than we imagine. Christmas music in

Christmas music
in particular
brings us
together in
a way that
sometimes
words just can't.

particular brings us together in a way that sometimes words just can't. Who doesn't hum along with Mariah Carey's "All I Want for Christmas Is You"? It seems that regardless of denomination or Christian tradition, many of us end our Christmas Eve worship experiences with some variation of "Silent Night."

How Do You Say "Poinsettia" Anyway?

On a large scale music bring us together, but on a smaller scale music can communicate something unique and intimate. Many of us might sing "Silent Night" by candlelight, but I imagine that your community sings it just a touch differently from the next. Do you sing accompanied by the organ or guitar, piano or a cappella? Do you hold your candles up during the last verse? Maybe your pastor processes out of the sanctuary before the song is over. These subtle differences become the unspoken oral tradition of your community, shaping your identity. Take a moment to consider the music at the end of your Christmas Eve service. What does it say about your community and how you understand that first Christmas? Does the conclusion of your gathering suggest a soft tenderness and intimacy of a first-time mother's embrace of a firstborn son? Maybe you end your service with a larger-than-life moment, trying to match the glory and grandeur of a heavenly host of angels. Maybe you end your worship in reverent quiet so that the night is truly silent.

Have you considered what someone outside of your community hears when they are with you? Is it a welcoming sound or noisy and abrasive, an unwelcoming nuisance? Sometimes it's hard to tell. Music not only shapes our identity and helps share our identity with others, it also reveals who is "in" and who is "out." This music doesn't necessarily need instruments or a noticeable melody. Our accents, the natural rise and fall of the melody of our speech, shape and form our idea of who is welcome and who might be looking from the outside in.

One morning while at seminary, I had the opportunity to lead a public prayer during a student worship service. The prayer wasn't particularly eloquent, though I wanted to communicate that I was no slouch when it comes to public speaking. Immediately following the service, someone met me outside the doors of the chapel and offered an interesting compliment. "You spoke really well for being a youth director from South Louisiana," he said. In my neighborhood we call compliments such as these "backhanded compliments." In his defense, if there is one, he was surprised that I didn't sound like I was from the New Orleans area. I jokingly said that I was running late and had to leave my gator-skin boots and banjo in the car.

The truth is I do have an accent, and so do you. Sometimes it's hard to hear until you speak with someone who doesn't have your same accent. Accents very quickly identify who you are, where you're from, and sometimes who's welcome and who isn't. Near the end of Matthew's Gospel, Peter's denial of Jesus is met with suspicion because of his accent. "A short time later those standing there came and said to Peter, 'You must be one of them. The way you talk gives you away'" (Matthew 26:73). Being in such a cosmopolitan city as Jerusalem during the festival of the Passover, Peter's Galilean accent must have been incredibly unique. In addition to a regional accent, did Jesus's followers use particular words or inflections that identified them with the Jesus movement? How unique is your "accent" as a Jesus follower?

Speech, more so than music, grabs our attention in the Christmas story. I'd love to tell you that the angel of the Lord appeared before shepherds with a multitude of instruments filling the night sky with a magnificent "Gloria" in "Hark the Herald Angels Sing," but sadly there's no music in the story. "Suddenly a great assembly of the heavenly forces was with the angel praising God. They *said*, 'Glory to God in heaven'" (Luke 2:13-14a, emphasis mine). The angels, or "heavenly forces," were praising and saying. "Praising," or *aineo*, means "speaking of the excellence of God." Much like God speaking creation into existence and calling it good, the angels continue to celebrate God's goodness at this foretaste of a new creation.

Luke uses this word surprisingly sparingly in his Gospel. Shortly after the shepherds "went quickly" to Bethlehem and revealed to Mary everything they had heard, Luke records, "The shepherds returned home, glorifying and praising [*aineo*] God for all they had heard and seen. Everything happened just as they had been told" (Luke 2:20). It is striking that the shepherds began mimicking or imitating the kind of language they received from the angels. It seems that good news is difficult to keep to oneself. It's infectious and joyful. It's like watching my daughter come out of the movie theater after seeing *Everything Everywhere All at Once*, which she rightfully claims is the "Best. Movie. Ever." It is impossible for her not to talk about her experience seeing this incredible film.

The next time Luke chooses to use *aineo* is during Jesus's triumphant entrance into Jerusalem in the last week of his earthly life:

> *As Jesus approached the road leading down from the Mount of Olives, the whole throng of his disciples began rejoicing. They praised [ainein] God with a loud voice because of all the mighty things they had seen. They said,*
>
> > *"Blessings on the king who comes in the name of the Lord.*
> > *Peace in heaven and glory in the highest heavens."*
>
> (Luke 19:37-38)

There were a multitude of angels and a multitude of disciples. Both the heavenly army and the army of disciples praised the power and might of God. Jesus's triumphant entry into Jerusalem on what we celebrate as Palm Sunday matches the magnitude that shocked sleepy shepherds at the beginning of Jesus's story. Jesus wasn't just entering Jerusalem. In Luke's mind, Jesus entering into Jerusalem should remind us of the grandeur of God entering into creation on the first noel. The melody of "Gloria in Excelsis Deo" should harmonize well with our "Hosanna." Praise (*aineo*), it seems, is reserved only for the most magnificent of moments in Jesus's story.

It should then come as no surprise to you that the final time "praising" is used in Luke's Gospel is at its conclusion: "They worshipped him and returned to Jerusalem overwhelmed with joy. And they were continuously in the temple praising [*aineo*] God" (Luke 24:52-53). Praise accompanied the angels in heaven announcing Jesus's birth. That same acknowledgment of God's excellence rang out in the streets of Jerusalem as Jesus approached the Temple. At the end of it all, that same praise has the final word before Luke begins his second volume detailing the birth and growth of the church.

How is it that you communicate this "excellence of God" in your faith community? Does praise look different this time of year? I would imagine that your community leaders spend more time in the sanctuary during Advent and Christmas than they do other times of the year—and of course they do! Luke reminds us that the announcement of Christ's birth carries more energy and jubilation than other moments on the calendar. Maybe this is why there's so much Christmas music playing on the radio, in the streets, and at end-of-the-year middle school band concerts. There is a rare and magnificent inbreaking of God's excellence that is so abundant it's hard to set aside.

MAJORING IN A MINOR KEY

When the shepherds had told the Holy Family all that they had heard, Mary "committed these things to memory and considered them carefully" (Luke 2:19). Everyone was amazed at what they heard, a fitting response for the kind of praising reserved for triumphant entries. But Mary was much more quiet and reflective. Considering doesn't seem to be the kind of thing that needs an audience or a megaphone. Her relatively hushed

49

The announcement of Christ's birth carries more energy and jubilation than other moments on the calendar.

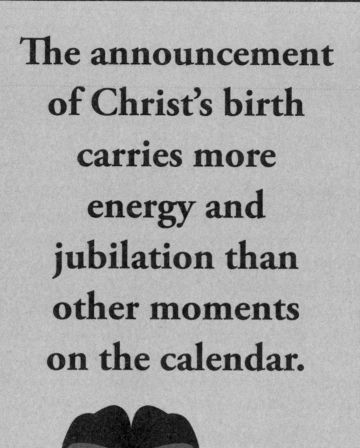

response is not passive or "meek and mild." Mary experienced an angel long before the shepherds' excitement. Mary experienced the prenatal leap for joy when she lodged with Elizabeth before her son John was born. She responded to the miraculous work of God with a song of justice and prophetic fervor, crying out through the ages saying, "He has shown strength with his arm. / He has scattered those with arrogant thoughts and proud inclinations. / He has pulled the powerful down from their thrones / and lifted up the lowly" (Luke 1:51-52). She isn't apathetic to the shepherds' excitement, but her quiet postpartum strength to treasure and consider reminds us that sometimes Christmas is much too loud.

What happens if our worship becomes quiet, or maybe we feel that God has become somehow silent? We read about angels from the realms of glory tearing apart the heavens to announce to unsuspecting shepherds that Christ is born; but what if it's all just too loud? Praising, offering words on the "excellence of God," is all well and good when life is full of joyful expectation, all of your Christmas-list gifts are able to be purchased, and planning family gatherings are smooth and conflict free. When things aren't going according to plan, or if the holidays bring up difficult memories, our praising can feel shallow at best. Our praise may feel disingenuous, put on, or at worst a wounding experience. When there is no peace in our praise, even the softest of sounds feel like a clanging, dissonant cymbal.

Sometimes silence can be deafening.

There have been two moments in my life when silence was the loudest thing in the room. In 2005, there was a couple excited to give birth to their firstborn child. The pregnancy wasn't as smooth as they had hoped, the child was coming earlier than expected, but there was little cause for alarm. The delivery was unremarkable, which is why a family member began to record the new mother and father's reactions at the moment of birth. Everything was just as you might imagine, until it wasn't. The doctor seemed to move a bit more quickly than she had before. Unfamiliar words began to ring out between nurses as if you were overhearing a quarterback change the play at the line of scrimmage. New instruments were being uncovered and prepped. And then in an instant the child was born, but "no crying he made."

The room rang with a silence that causes every muscle in your body to tighten. Like a descant above beeping machines, clanging instruments, and whirling staff, the voice of the mother cut through the chaos saying, "Is everything OK?" No one answered. The mother, more panicked, asked again, "Is everything OK?" Again, there was no answer because the staff was working with a singular focus, unable to be deterred by anything else, even a mother's plea. The mother finally questioned to anyone who would listen, "Why isn't he crying? Why don't I hear him crying?" And then, as if the child could hear his mother's agony, he cried, the room exhaled, and everything was OK. Not every story in the delivery room ends with good news, but in this case, everything was good. Next year this child will be graduating high school ready to start a new journey of his own.

The other instance was back when I was a pastoral intern. The church staff got word that a member was in the hospital with a newly diagnosed aggressive form of cancer. The diagnosis wasn't good. The young woman's health faded quickly. This was the one hospital visit to which my pastoral supervisor, Dr. James Howell, denied me access, and for good reason. I was young. I was learning. My involvement would not have been helpful. The stakes were far too high between pastor and parishioner for this to be a clinic. Not long after we heard she was sick, the young woman died, leaving behind a husband and two precious children. I sat in the balcony for the funeral. Dr. Howell's words were eloquent and honest, wrenching and hopeful, but his witness is not what I hold from that moment. As the casket was recessing away from the chancel, the woman's older daughter reached out and said, "Mama."

There wasn't any oxygen left in the room after every soul in the church gasped with an unspeakable sorrow. No one moved for what seemed an eternity. The silence was poignant as if you could hear hearts breaking one by one as the procession moved past each pew. I can still hear that silence, but I imagine it pales in comparison with the perpetual silence her husband and children still hear. Sometimes Christmas is far too loud.

Later in the week, I mentioned to James how the silence in the chapel was unnerving. He told me a story that he recorded in his work, *The Beauty of the Word*:

> When I was in seminary, I had a close friend who suffered terribly yet courageously from cystic fibrosis. During one particularly bleak night at the Duke Medical Center, I was sitting with her and her mother, agonizing with her as she wearily fought for the most shallow of breaths.... When I stood up to leave, her mother was standing over by the window, looking out at—well, at

53

nothing at all. . . . Pitifully I asked, "Would you like for me to say a prayer?" Her barely audible reply numbed me: "Pray if you wish. Nobody is listening." . . . When a mother sits in hospital rooms over the years . . . she knows the darkness. . . . Who are you to fix all the mothers . . . whose lives have been flayed, whose wounds are gaping, who will cry out against God, with or without you? . . . We name the ache. We articulate the brokenheartedness. We say what people have not let themselves say out loud. . . . Truth always looks to Jesus—and especially to his cross—and is content in its shadow.[1]

Sometimes we need to sit in the silence to listen to someone else's heart. Mary, the mother of Jesus, seems unapologetically unafraid to rest in this quiet place. She is wholly counter to the holy encounter the shepherds report, and she lingers in this liminal space, holding it for the rest of us. Eight days after Jesus is born, Mary and Joseph presented Jesus in the Temple. I can imagine there was a quiet moment when Mary handed Jesus to Simeon who said:

> *"Now, master, let your servant go in peace according to your word,*
> *because my eyes have seen your salvation.*
> *You prepared this salvation in the presence of all peoples.*
> *It's a light for revelation to the Gentiles*
> *and a glory for your people Israel."*
>
> *(Luke 2:29-32)*

Mary and Joseph were amazed at what was being said about him, but this amazement was short lived. Simeon blessed them and said to his mother, "This boy is assigned to be the cause of the

54

Mary, the mother
of Jesus, seems
unapologetically
unafraid to
rest in this
quiet place.

falling and rising of many in Israel and to be a sign that generates opposition so that the inner thoughts of many will be revealed. And a sword will pierce your innermost being too" (Luke 2:34-35). We aren't told how Mary reacted to this prophecy, but she's already well acquainted with the marriage between amazement and terror. It seems that seeing an angel appear and say, "Rejoice, favored one!" (Luke 1:28) is not for the faint of heart. How pierced will her soul be? Would it be the kind of anxiety parents feel when their child is in the spotlight? The falling and rising of many certainly will garner great attention. Will her child be shamed through scandal or be despised as a failed military leader? We ask the question in song every year around Christmas, but how much did Mary know anyway?

This is almost the last we hear of Mary in Luke's story. But not quite. The ending of Luke 2 details a time when Jesus was twelve years old, and his family went to Jerusalem for the Passover festival. Somehow Jesus was separated from the group, and they began traveling home without him. After three days of searching, they found him in the Temple having conversation with the teachers there. Again this child brought about amazement, but also great frustration. Mary says, "Child, why have you treated us like this?" (Luke 2:48). I think the tradition has remembered a rather censored version of this exchange. As a parent myself, after losing and finding my child over the course of three days, the language used wouldn't be nearly as formal and polite. I imagine there's a lot left unsaid in this exchange. Why have you treated us like this?

Mary's indignant question points to the awe and anguish that attend Jesus's arrival. Why have you treated us like this? Why are you at the same time conceived in holiness, and yet carry the potential of such shame when an unwed mother announces that she's pregnant? The heavens are torn apart, angels announce your birth to shepherds, and yet there isn't any "place for [us] in the guestroom"? Your cousin John leapt in the womb at the mere mention of your presence, and we somehow pass over you during the Passover. Why do you treat us like this? There is such magnificence and pain, praise with pondering. Is this what Simeon meant when he said Mary's soul would be pierced? How much else will she need to endure? And then, for the rest of the story, Mary is silent, leaving us to ponder what she treasured.

SINGING A NEW SONG

One of the prophesies typically read during the Advent season reads:

> The things announced in the past—look—they've already happened,
>> but I'm declaring new things.
>> Before they even appear,
>> I tell you about them.
>
> Sing to the LORD a new song!
>> Sing his praise from the ends of the earth!
>>> (Isaiah 42:9-10a)

The former things have passed away, and new things are on the horizon. And yet, like Mary, somehow we can feel caught in the middle of those two truths. Singing a new song isn't easy. Sometimes a new song brings with it a dissonance that is unacceptable to those who have memorized the old song. It's disorienting, jarring, and soul piercing. Jesus offers a new song that brings joy to shepherds and makes the Herods of the world quake. This new song opens the ears of the deaf and the eyes of the blind, but the healing happens on the Sabbath, which creates discord among the religious elite. This new song talks about the last being first and the Gentile being welcomed and eunuchs being baptized. This new song sounds like the change from the Temple treasury cascading onto the stone floor because Jesus has overturned the table. This new song looks at Lazarus's tomb and says he is only sleeping. It is a song that the Pharisees and the Romans and the Herodians refuse to sing. It is a song that the zealots and the powerful and the proud must stop at all costs. There is a dissonance between this new song and the precarious melody of original and not-so-original sin. If they try to occupy the same space at the same time it sounds like a siren, which can get your attention, but your ears can't handle it for long.

Do you hear what I hear when we "listen" to Jesus? The magnificence and suffering both ring true, but they aren't dissonant; rather they are leading. A leading tone in music is a particular pitch in a certain key that leads you to finding home, or the root of the key. For example, sing to yourself the ending of "Joy to the World":

> And heaven and nature sing,
> And heaven and nature sing.
> And heaven, and heaven, and nature…

Do you feel how hard it is not to complete the line? Do you feel that tension? The second syllable of "nature" in the last line lands on a leading tone. It's almost irresistibly pushing you to the "home" of the key signature. That's what a leading tone does. It creates tension in the melody, but for the purpose of leading you home. The things that are passing away, as Isaiah prophesied so long ago, want us to perpetually live in dissonance with Christ's holy melody, not the tension of the leading tone. When we fail to love our neighbor, pursue power over people, seek wealth over someone's worth, our soul is restless because it isn't being led home. This is why sin is so tempting. It's easy. It sounds like it fits in the song, but it doesn't actually go anywhere, contribute anything, or push us where we need to be. The tension of the leading tone is what Mary treasured and pondered. Sometimes we stay in the leading tone because we just aren't ready to sing ourselves home. Silence can take over because we are afraid of what it might mean to be rooted and grounded in love. Heaven and nature...sing in the person of Jesus. Paul tells us that faith comes by hearing, but maybe faith comes by singing, too.

Eventually the tension gives way. We can't perpetually lean into a leading tone. This is why God blessed us with harmony. When heaven and nature sing together, when the fully divine and fully human melodies come together in the person of Jesus, we find our harmonic peace. Peace isn't passive. It's a hard-fought reality sometimes reachable only through unspeakable lament. Do you hear what I hear? Do you hear what your neighbor hears? What melody do you offer with which your neighbor might harmonize? Sometimes it's a holy silence that makes room for a new song. The song we are called to sing is beautiful and powerful. On the night Jesus was born, the heavens were opened and the shepherds saw a multitude of angels praising God. The song of praise continued with a multitude of disciples as Jesus entered into Jerusalem announcing his Messiahship to the proud and powerful. This song of praise resonated in the hearts of the early church as they held everything in common, broke bread together, and met the needs of all. Maybe that's why there's so much music this time of year. Words alone cannot contain God's abundance Jesus revealed to the world. We sing, we dance, we celebrate, we treasure, we ponder, and sometimes we remain silent. Imagine for a moment Christmas without music. It almost seems impossible...

Words alone cannot
contain God's
abundance Jesus
revealed to the world.
We sing, we dance,
we celebrate, we
treasure, we ponder,
and sometimes we
remain silent.

QUESTIONS

1. What do you imagine the first Christmas sounded like? What sounds would have accompanied Jesus's birth? What did the shepherds hear before the angel appeared to them?

2. How would you describe the soundtrack of your life? What do you hear regularly—from music to everyday noises? How does the soundtrack change in the weeks before Christmas?

3. How do you praise and communicate the "excellence of God" in your faith community? How do you do this differently during Advent?

4. How does Mary's "considering" show us the value of silence? How does silence point to the mystery of the Incarnation?

5. Where do you see the new song of Advent clashing with the old songs of our world?

CHAPTER THREE

DO YOU TASTE WHAT I TASTE?

CHAPTER THREE

Do You Taste What I Taste?

Taste and see how good the LORD is!
The one who takes refuge in him is truly happy!
(Psalm 34:8)

Do you have that one thing that makes it finally feel like Christmas is around the corner? Maybe seeing the lights on the Christmas tree or the department store decorations signal the season. Maybe for you it's the first time the radio station becomes a 24-hour Jingle Bell jukebox that says to you that you need to have your presents under the tree? My mother and I share December birthdays, so Christmas was a relatively short season in my household growing up. Ideally the tree goes up after my birthday on the eleventh and comes down before my mother's on the twenty-ninth. This brief window wasn't always the case, but we usually tried for it. And I triple-dog dare you to wrap my mother's birthday presents in the leftover green and red wrapping paper. You have been warned.

It takes a while for me to get into the Christmas spirit. It's hard to avoid seeing the yard decorations, and it's even more impossible to close my ears to the ubiquitous carols that seem to be all around us. They just don't do it for me. There's nothing wrong with the seasonal sights and sounds, of course, but there's one thing I like to save to signal that it's time to get the manger ready. I'd love to tell you that this one thing is dramatic, life changing, rooted in service and devotion, but it's not. I am not too ashamed to say that when the Starbucks gingerbread latte hits my lips, it feels as if Santa himself called my name from the barista station. I name and claim this guilty pleasure, and before you roll your eyes at the shallow and simple luxury of gingerbready goodness, think about the tastes and aromas that you enjoy. I'm sure there's a food, drink, or dish that makes your heart say to itself, "It's time to deck the halls."

It's like that fantastic scene at the end of Disney/Pixar's *Ratatouille*, a movie about an ordinary rat named Remy who loves to cook and who decides to pursue that dream. In one of my favorite scenes, a food critic—Anton Ego, a cold, frail, no-nonsense kind of guy—comes into the restaurant to render his verdict. Of all the dishes they could serve, Remy decides to make ratatouille, a French peasant's dish. The decision to serve ratatouille makes everyone nervous. For someone so important and powerful, especially someone who can with the stroke of his pen define your future success or failure, making something so seemingly simple seems irresponsible. Ignoring the apprehension from his friends, Remy dishes up the ratatouille. Ego is initially apathetic and unimpressed, neither surprised nor disgusted at the entrée. But when Ego takes his first bite of the dish, his mind immediately hearkens back to his boyhood home kitchen table where his mom comforts him with a warm bowl of ratatouille. The cold critic drops his pen, symbolically laying down his pretension and self-importance. His life is forever changed by the meal.

The sights and sounds of the season are everywhere, but taste and its related sense, smell, are underrated. The Christmas story offers us a vivid picture of shepherds and angels, dreams and visions, but doesn't really tell us anything about the sense of taste. Our sense of taste is unique, individual, subjective, and powerful. Taste can offer a sense of wonder or the comfort of home. Taste is a gift. Food doesn't have to taste good, but it does, and therefore taste reminds us of grace. God doesn't have to forgive. God doesn't have to be merciful. God didn't have to empty the divine and walk with us, use our language, or eat our food, but God did. The simple joy of tasting something delicious causes us involuntarily to stop, breathe, and be thankful. That sounds like the gospel to me. The psalmist's advice to "taste and see how good the Lord is" isn't about salty, sweet, or savory, but it is about what satisfies.

Taste is a gift.
Food doesn't have
to taste good,
but it does, and
therefore taste
reminds us
of grace.

THE FIRST COMMUNION

During the COVID-19 pandemic, especially when things were shuttered, out of necessity my family began to cook at home more than we were accustomed to. It's not that we didn't cook at home before, but when you're a family of six with a hundred after-school activities, and pizza and burgers are closer to you than the grocery store, grabbing something on the way to somewhere was common. During quarantine, the grocery store was often the only open establishment, and that forced us into a different way of being. Has necessity ever forced you into a different rhythm or schedule? It could be something as simple as a change in shift schedule or the change to daylight saving time. Some changes are more significant. I remember when I went to college and could choose my own schedule, I stacked everything as early in the morning as possible. For an entire year, my classes were over by 12:30 p.m., which meant I could kill lots of time in the cafeteria, and then nap for most of the afternoon. To this day I have a hard time keeping my eyes open in the early afternoon.

Maybe the change of routine is dramatic and life-changing. Maybe someone you love received a terminal diagnosis, or the company is downsizing and you've had to retire earlier than expected. One of the biggest changes in my routine happened when we had our first child. I'm not sure what I was anticipating, but I can say with confidence that I was not prepared. My oldest didn't sleep for more than three hours at a time for the first five months of her life. The first time she did have a stretch long enough to not be considered parental torture was around Christmas. We traveled to visit family, and for whatever reason, she decided to sleep a whopping five hours one night. We called it the Christmas miracle.

Our sleep patterns certainly changed, but so did our eating. I've grown to appreciate the relationship between eating and our daily rhythm. Growing up, the schedule was expected and meals helped track the day. I ate breakfast before school, lunch in the school cafeteria at an extraordinarily early time, a midafternoon snack that would rival an adult's full meal, and then dinner around the table with the family before sneaking some kind of snack into my room before bed. Over the years the schedule changed from one extreme to the other. In some seasons I've eaten like a Hobbit from *Lord of the Rings*, having multiple meals a day only a few hours apart. At other times I've counted calories, kept food logs, and eaten very specific diets. Never has the relationship between eating and a daily rhythm been so significant than we had our first child.

People may tell you that your life changes when you get married, but that change pales in comparison to when you bring a baby into your home. Isabelle had to feed every three hours for the first several months of her life. We had to divide our daily and evening activities into three-hour cycles, and that was the maximum window. After the baby nursed, she had to be held upright for thirty minutes because of her reflux, and then there's changing the diaper, putting her back to sleep or moving into the living room for tummy time. It wasn't long before the whole process began again. It felt like there wasn't much time to do anything, and I wasn't even the one doing the feeding!

It has taken me an embarrassingly long time to realize that between angels, shepherds, livestock, and all the hubbub that the Gospels record about Jesus's birth, at some point Mary nursed Jesus. The Gospels say nothing about what I assume to be a holy and intimate connection between mother and child. I'm not surprised that this detail is overlooked. Scripture unfortunately glosses over the whole event. Luke reports, "She gave birth to her firstborn child, a son, wrapped him snugly, and laid him in a manger, because there was no place for them in the guestroom" (Luke 2:7). Matthew reports even less, going from "This is how the birth of Jesus Christ took place" to "After Jesus was born in Bethlehem in the territory of Judea during the rule of King Herod…" without announcing a specific moment that Jesus had been born (Matthew 1:18; 2:1a). Could it be with all the divine images of dreams and angels, shepherds and stars, that the actual birth seems far too human to report? Perhaps the male authors of the Gospels didn't know what to say, or they were too entrenched in their own perspective to recognize the omission.

Did Mary struggle to give birth? Was Joseph by her side, or was he keeping watch like the shepherds to fend off any danger for such a vulnerable moment? I wonder who the unnamed heroes of this story might be? Did Mary have a midwife at her side, like Shiphrah and Puah in Exodus, who saved the lives of Hebrew babies by disobeying Pharoah's command to kill any boys who were born (Exodus 1:15-22)? Without their strength, courage, and holy deception, Exodus may have been a very short book. Could it be that Mary was alone? I can't imagine the fear and anxiety that accompanies labor, especially for a first-time mother.

Scripture is silent on the details of Jesus's birth and nursing. Maybe it's the humanness of it all. We seem to have an easy time accepting Jesus's divinity. It's the human parts that make us uncomfortable. Christmas is a time for polishing the brass, getting out the fine china for the staff party, and putting on the garish sweater that you'll only wear once. Although birth is something we all share, it's best not to muck things up with talk of a mother's body exposed, the pain of labor, and the messiness of afterbirth. We don't want to offend our polite Christian sensibilities with talk of breastfeeding, let alone allowing mothers to breastfeed in church. During a 2018 Vatican baptism ceremony in the Sistine Chapel, Pope Francis remarked, "'Babies have their own dialect.... If one starts to cry the others will follow, like in an orchestra.' He said that if the babies were 'starting a concert' of crying because they were hungry, mothers should 'go ahead and feed them,' for this too is a 'language of love.'"[1] And yet I assume this "language of love" is still asked to be censored, covered, or made discrete.

We sing, "Little Lord Jesus, no crying he makes," because Mary offered Jesus his first meal. The vulnerability and intimacy of that moment just might have had the power to bring creation to its knees in praise and thanksgiving. It's a holy moment that, in a way, looks forward to the Last Supper. Mary offered her body as nourishment to the One who, some thirty years later, would offer his body for ours in the breaking of the bread. From the beginning of Jesus's life, there has been a holy reciprocity of food in the most divine and intimate sense. The church during the medieval period didn't shy away from the mystery and beauty of Mary

Mary offered her
body as nourishment
to the One who,
some thirty years
later, would offer
his body for ours
in the breaking
of the bread.

nursing Jesus. The "Nursing Madonna," or *Galaktotrophousa*, was an iconographic tradition until the Council of Trent in the mid-sixteenth century when it began to be discouraged. The icons of Mary nursing are meant to invite meditation on the connection between Mary's nourishment of Christ, and Christ's nourishment of us through Holy Communion.

To find out more about the connection between nursing and Communion, I went to St. Jude's, a Roman Catholic church just north of my congregation. With celebrations for the Annunciation, immaculate conception, Magnificat, Epiphany, and *Quasimodogeniti* (which is related to Easter, but means "like newborn infants"), I reasoned that surely there is a word in the Roman Catholic church for a teaching so profound. I explained my fascination with the reciprocity between Mary sustaining Jesus and Jesus sustaining us, wondering if the church recognizes that this perhaps is the first Eucharist. Surprisingly, I learned that there isn't an official recognition of Jesus's first feeding or Jesus's weaning. (There should be, and maybe this tradition begins with your congregation!) I did discover something, though. I was in Father Karl's office on the feast day of the immaculate conception, the day the Roman Catholic church recognizes that Mary was conceived. I felt the Holy Spirit telling me, "Listen. Stop. Pay attention." It was an invitation to me to consider a story that isn't mine—to regard an experience that I've never had, and will never have, as an example of the Holy.

Considering the sense of taste and the experience of Jesus's first meal reminds us that Christmas is so much more vulnerable and intimate than the sights and sounds suggest.

DIFFERENT FLAVORS

I'm ashamed it took me so long to recognize such a simple, vulnerable, and profound truth of the Christmas story that seems to be so overlooked, disregarded, or hushed. Maybe this is the first time you're considering the importance of Mary sustaining Christ for us, or maybe you've known this for quite a while, and you're just waiting for the rest of us to catch up. The Christmas story reminds us to take a moment and consider someone else's perspective. Or maybe more accurately, to recognize the voices that have been overlooked, forgotten, or silenced. In Matthew's Gospel we receive an inner glance into Joseph's experience of Jesus's birth. Mary doesn't ever speak. Conversely, Luke offers us great detail on Mary's experience, and Joseph never speaks. One Gospel remembers magi; another Gospel records shepherds. In one Gospel the family is already in Bethlehem, and in the other they travel for the census. The stories are true, and they disagree on the details.

I wish it were as simple as a single portrait. The second-century theologian, Tatian, tried to make it easy on us by synthesizing all four Gospels into one single story, but the church said no. Matthew, Mark, Luke, and John all offer us different angles, different perspectives, and different flavors of the one we call Christ, the Lord. The way each Gospel begins gives us the flavor of what's to come.

Mark, the oldest Gospel, says, "The beginning of the good news about Jesus Christ, God's Son." That's not even a complete sentence. There's no verb, but it reveals a lot of what Mark's understanding of Jesus is. The way Mark tells the Gospel reveals Jesus to be constantly on the move. It's an incomplete sentence almost as if there wasn't time to write it all down. The Book of Mark is also about what's called the "Messianic Secret." The disciples recognize Jesus as the Messiah only gradually, and they misunderstand initially what this means, and Jesus instructs them to keep the matter a secret for much of the story. For Mark to include "good news" and "God's Son" in the first verse is a comment on the authority of Caesar. Good news was to come from Rome, and the emperor was the Son of God. Jesus is on the move, impatient, and works in secret.

Matthew's Gospel offers us a different picture. Matthew begins with, "A record of the ancestors of Jesus Christ, son of David, son of Abraham." In Mark, Jesus appears out of nowhere with no backstory or history. Matthew wants to make sure Jesus is rooted in a real time and a real place. Also unlike Mark, Matthew offers a birth narrative, revealing that Jesus is the son of David and the son of Abraham, which means that Jesus is both a king from the Davidic line but is also sacrificial as was Isaac, Abraham's son. This sacrificial king looks like a new Moses, offering a re-narration of the law and a systematic mission leading to Jerusalem. By the end of the story, Jesus is the judge of the nations calling the disciples to baptize the world.

Luke's story brings the Gospel to a more intimate place.

Many people have already applied themselves to the task of compiling an account of the events that have been fulfilled among us. They used what the original

76

eyewitnesses and servants of the word handed down to us. Now, after having investigated everything carefully from the beginning, I have also decided to write a carefully ordered account for you, most honorable Theophilus. I want you to have confidence in the soundness of the instruction you have received.

(Luke 1:1-4)

Luke is writing to Theophilus, which means, "Friend of God"; so in a sense, Luke is writing to you. Luke is less concerned with baptizing the nations than he is concerned with the baptism of you. Luke gives us the birth narrative with which we are most familiar, with angels and shepherds and Gabriel visiting Mary. Luke presumably writing to a Greek individual also shows us that he's writing to a Gentile audience, so he's writing to those who are less familiar with Judaism. Therefore, Jesus in Luke's Gospel is very concerned with outsiders and outcasts and healing. For example, all of the Gospels record that Jesus was crucified with two other people. Some of the Gospels record that they were criminals. Only Luke's Gospel remembers that one of them turned to Jesus and said, "Remember me when you come into your kingdom," to which Jesus replied, "I assure you that today you will be with me in paradise" (Luke 23:42-43). It's only in Luke's Gospel that we have the redemption of the criminal as part of the story's culmination. The parable of the prodigal son is only in Luke's Gospel. There is a thread of redemption of those whom society thinks are unworthy.

In Mark, Jesus is a mysterious miracle worker. In Matthew, Jesus is the great rabbi or teacher, re-narrating the Jewish law. In

Luke, Jesus is friend to outcasts and outsiders, concerned with redemption of those not included in the faith. And then there's John's Gospel. Matthew, Mark, and Luke tend to agree on the whole of what Jesus said, where Jesus went, and the general rhythm of Jesus's life. They are called the "Synoptic Gospels" because they are more or less in sync with each other. John's Gospel is quite different. John's Gospel begins with "In the beginning was the Word / and the Word was with God / and the Word was God." John's Gospel is less about where Jesus went and what Jesus did as it is about who Jesus is, and this is told through a series of I AM statements: I am the light of the world; I am the bread of life; I am the way, the truth, and the life.

These different Gospels offer different "flavors" of the banquet that is Jesus. Again, the film *Ratatouille* helps us understand this. Early in the movie, Remy is talking with his brother, Emile, about the magnificence and mystery of flavor. He takes a bite of some cheese, and in his imagination, he hears samba music playing with yellow swirls dancing about. Then he samples a strawberry to Parisian background music and red squiggles and circles. He then gets the idea to eat both at the same time. After he bites there is Parisian samba music playing to red and yellow squiggles and swirls revealing a new flavor altogether. It's not that the color became orange and the music independent and distinct, rather the different flavors complemented each other to create a unique experience. When we read the Gospels together, comparing and contrasting the different flavors of the story, we aren't building something new and independent from the sources; rather we experience a fuller picture of both the individual Gospel and how the Gospel contributes to the overall picture of Jesus. For example, one of the things I most appreciate about United Methodism is the call to read Scripture through tradition, reason, and experience. We feast upon God's word, but the different spices of tradition, reason, and experience unlock the flavor, so to speak. Interpreting Scripture through tradition, reason, and experience adds a complexity to the Bible that might be missed if we weren't intentionally savoring what it has to say.

Have you ever been to a wine or bourbon tasting? I've rolled my eyes a time or two when someone sips a fine wine and notices a hint of black currant balanced with a floral rose built upon a foundation of an oaken barrel from Tuscany. Not long ago some friends and I went to a bourbon tasting outside of Austin, Texas, and with some guidance, I was astounded at how I could pick up hints of flavors and smells, and how those flavors and smells changed over time during our dinner. When reading Scripture patiently, letting the different flavors dance with and against each other, we finally begin to understand Scripture's depth; and what a feast it is!

DOUBLE-BOILING CHOCOLATE

Almost every year my wife and I host the church staff in our home for our end-of-the-year Christmas gathering. What we lack in a fancy home we make up for with a fancy dinner. Weeks before the staff comes over I practice the main dish over and over again. Is the marinade for the pork tenderloin balanced? Would a Caesar salad or field greens make the plate? Does the chocolate

When reading
Scripture patiently,
letting the different
flavors dance with
and against each
other, we finally
begin to understand
Scripture's depth;
and what a feast it is!

mousse have the perfect consistency? I have to practice these things because cooking for others is a special, personal activity— one that I haven't always gotten right. In college I wanted to make my wife, Christie, some chocolate truffles. The instructions said to double boil the chocolate with a half inch of water. So, I poured about a half inch of water in my saucepan, brought it to a boil, and added chocolate chips, let it cool, and then boiled it all over again to begin this soon-to-be amazing dessert. Except, the chocolate never came together. It became a flavorless chocolate soup, but I simply thought I had happened upon a happy accident of innovation.

She was so polite after tasting what I thought was a spot-on new creation that I had made. After she admitted that she was less than impressed, I explained what I had done. After she caught her breath from the chorus of seemingly endless laughter that ensued, she had just enough strength to call me "Amelia Bedelia" before explaining to me how I messed up. I now know that a double boiler is a pan for melting chocolate and not a description of how to melt chocolate. (I was curious how the recipe author knew, without detailing the size of the saucepan, how much a half-inch of water would be.) Boiling chocolate twice with water, a truffle does not make.

Cooking for someone is a vulnerable and intimate act that reminds me of the mystery of Christmas. The Gospels offer us the different flavors: mysterious miracle worker, great teacher, redeemer of outcasts, and the Word of God. Then you turn the page to Paul's letters. Even before the Gospels were penned down, between something like AD 70-110, Paul's letters present us with

81

who this Messiah is. The oldest formal worshipful picture of who Jesus is is called the "Christ Hymn" in Philippians 2:5-11—

Adopt the attitude that was in Christ Jesus:

> *Though he was in the form of God,*
> > *he did not consider being equal with God*
> > *something to exploit.*
> *But he emptied himself*
> > *by taking the form of a slave*
> > *and by becoming like human beings.*
> *When he found himself in the form of a human,*
> > *he humbled himself by becoming obedient to*
> > *the point of death,*
> > *even death on a cross.*
> *Therefore, God highly honored him*
> > *and gave him a name above all names,*
> *so that at the name of Jesus everyone*
> > *in heaven, on earth, and under the earth*
> > *might bow*
> > *and every tongue confess*
> > > *that Jesus Christ is Lord, to the glory of*
> > > *God the Father.*

Jesus was in the form of God. When you can't see what's under the surface, look to the birds. Looking to Jesus is looking to God. The church teaches that God and Jesus are made of the same stuff, or *homoousion*, as mentioned in the Nicene Creed developed in the fourth century. Whatever makes up God also makes up Jesus. How beautifully ambiguous… "Though he was in the form of God, / he did not consider being equal with God something to exploit. / But he emptied himself."

For a moment I want you to notice a parallel. In the first chapter I talked about creation, about how God looked upon creation and saw that it was good; but God was looking at creation as creator. Try as we might, we cannot comprehend the chasm between creator and creation. We cannot perceive what it means for anything to exist outside of creation. God knows we can't. This is what Christmas is about. God "emptied" the divine so that God could see, hear, and touch from the perspective of creation. God's first action of creation finds a parallel here in Philippians. In the beginning when God began creating the heavens and the earth, God created with a "let there be." "Let there be" isn't passive, but it's also not domineering or coercive. There is a humility in God's creative work in the sense that God wasn't creating for God; rather God was creating for everything that wasn't. There is great humility in God to make room for that which is not God. Here in the Philippians "Christ Hymn," there is a word about creation claiming that Jesus is of the same substance as God, and then immediately there is a humbling. Christ is of the same divine substance, but not as a means of exploitation. Christ emptied the divine self for everything that wasn't Christ.

This emptying and humility has huge implications for what we understand about God's love. Christmas teaches that God had to rely on humanity in order to save humanity. In short, Jesus had parents. Jesus had to be taught and fed and brought to the synagogue, and I'm sure put in time-out a time or two. Yes, the Lord of lords and the King of kings, fully divine, and also fully human. As Stanley Hauerwas wrote, "To be human is to be vulnerable, but to be a baby is to be vulnerable in a manner we spend a lifetime denying."[2] Mary offering herself as nourishment to the One who offers himself for our nourishment reveals that God is more faithful toward humanity than we are toward God or toward each other.

IT'S NEVER A TABLE FOR ONE

To my knowledge there is no record of Jesus eating alone. When we see him eating, it's always with someone. Maybe that's the real lesson here, that eating is a communal activity. For whom is your table set? Maybe someone in your circle is desperately lonely, needing to know she or he has a place at your table and in your life. We have a saying in my hometown: "We don't eat to live, we live to eat!" There's actually something quite beautiful about this. We are so used to an "eat to live" world where food must be fast, catered only to me and my schedule, instead of a "live to eat" world where we make table fellowship a priority.

Children have a way of humbling us into a good place. When you have a baby, you can't just add an extra chicken tender or make more chili. You must introduce food slowly and methodically to check for allergies and preferences, making sure not to feed her too many carrots so that she doesn't turn orange, and double-checking that you don't accidentally feed her an entire jar of prunes (that was a memorable day). Food and relationship are inseparable. The menu matters when you gather around a common table, and especially when you haven't had the best track record in the kitchen.

When I was in college, my wife's grandmother gave me her food dehydrator because she knew how much I liked beef jerky, so I started making my own. It was fantastic. After several rounds of making different kinds of beef jerky, I thought to myself, "You know what you never see in stores? Chicken jerky." So, I laid out a pound of raw chicken strips on the dehydrator, waited about a day and a half, and then sampled the first tender. It was so good that I then went on to eat the entire pound of raw chicken that had been sitting out for a day and a half. Needless to say, several hours later I was not feeling well. Christie came over to the apartment and I called my mother. The conversation went something like this: "Mom, I think I have a stomach bug. I've never felt this terrible." "Was it something you ate?" "I don't think so. I mean, I did eat a pound of chicken jerky, but that can't be it" … [silence] "Chicken jerky?! Son … that's just natural selection trying to take you out of the gene pool. Get to the hospital." Of course I protested. I couldn't go to the hospital! LSU was kicking off at 2:30 the next day. I'm not missing the game.

I missed the game.

I didn't love cooking when I was younger. It felt like a chore. Eventually, and mostly because of the pandemic, I began to fall in love with it. Food is such a part of the culture in my home area of New Orleans. Cajun, Creole, Caribbean, and Latin American influences give New Orleans a unique flavor that you just won't find anywhere else. Food is a part of every culture everywhere. I'm sure if I were to ask you right now if you have a story about a favorite meal growing up, or a family recipe that is important to you, or a smell or a taste that immediately transports you back home, you would recall several. Both of my parents were familiar with the kitchen, so it makes sense that I might discover an affinity for the culinary arts. My mother cooked during the week, and my father would cook over the weekends. Both would offer what became some of my favorite dishes. I would ask for my mother's manicotti every time I was home visiting. My mother's beef and vegetable soup really is the best beef and vegetable soup I've ever had.

While my mother's dishes were practical, setting the rhythm for the week, my dad would often spend the weekends experimenting with different dishes. My mother would make a pot roast, but my dad would make "pizza plops," which was a failed pizza recipe. The crust never set, so it was kind of like pizza-themed soup. As kids, we loved it because we thought it was so clever. There are no mistakes, only happy accidents. My dad would make "hot dogs from another planet," which were hot dogs but you forgot hot dog buns, so you take regular bread, put toothpicks through it, put them in the oven with cheese, and eventually they look like space ships. To this day, almost every weekend my dad is trying a different recipe with different ingredients. My dad is a chemist, and very early on I was taught that cooking is just chemistry you can eat.

This may be a silly question, but sometimes those are the most fun. Did Jesus have a favorite meal? Was there a particular food that brought him joy? Did Jesus ever complain to Mary that they had too much hummus? Scripture doesn't really tell us what Jesus ate. We know that Jesus ate the Passover meal, and Jesus ate bread and fish, but outside of that, Scripture really doesn't detail what Jesus ate. We can assume that Jesus ate Mediterranean food. It's fascinating to think that Jesus probably ate lamb and grape leaves and probably hummus, and it all seems beautifully mundane.

Did he have something like red beans on Monday, taco Tuesdays, and so on? We know that he cooked. After the Resurrection when the disciples had returned to fishing, Jesus was on the lakeshore cooking fish and invited them to breakfast, and that's how they knew it was the Lord. They knew it was Jesus because he served them breakfast. If Jesus came to you today and asked you to join him for dinner, how would you respond? Would you cook at home? Would you go to a five-star restaurant? Would you keep it quiet so you could maximize your alone time with Jesus? Would you take him to a food truck? Would you look at your calendar and say, "Aw, geez, I have a super full day today. Maybe next week?" Maybe the better question is, How many times has Jesus already invited you to dinner? How many times has the Holy Spirit tried to get our attention at the dinner table, but we were consumed by anything but the food or the company in front of us?

I don't know about your household, but growing up our household was a zoo. When I would come home from school, Mom would be doing laundry while stirring dinner, my sister would be practicing the piano while practicing ballet. My other sister would be watching TV and listening to the radio while doing homework. I would go and play video games while practicing voice lessons while daydreaming. Sometimes we fill up our schedules each day, not because there are things we have to do but because, when we are busy, brothers and sisters don't have to play with one another, husbands and wives don't have to talk with each other, families don't have to sit around a table and talk about their days. When we have to wait, when we have to slow down, we become vulnerable because there are no longer any distractions.

Cooking takes time, and it's supposed to. When we slow down, when we become vulnerable by waiting, we are making room in our souls for desire. This is what happens when a child sits in front of the presents under the tree, staring, dreaming of what lies under the red and green and gold paper. It may seem like the child is wasting time, but that doesn't mean there's not an important lesson to be learned. By sitting there, wasting time, slowing down, the child is making room for desire, allowing the excitement and wonder and imagination to settle into his or her being. The beautiful thing about Advent is that we are given permission to do the same thing, to slow down, to waste time, to allow room in our souls for desire, to sit and waste time with an old friend, to again feel the desire of friendship, to sit and waste time with your spouse, to again feel the desire within marriage, to sit and waste time with your siblings, to feel the desire of family, to sit in the sanctuary, staring at the Advent wreath, getting lost in the chrismon tree, kneeling at the table, in order to be filled with the desire to see the radiant beams of the Christ Child's holy face.

We cannot survive without food, and eating is meant to be communal. There is such a connected depth between food and culture and identity. One summer my family decided to eat a meal once a week that was either from a different country or ethnicity. The only catch was that we had to interview someone

Cooking takes time, and it's supposed to. When we slow down, when we become vulnerable by waiting, we are making room in our souls for desire.

who had a relationship with that particular cuisine. For example, the first week we started small and had fish and chips, which my children had never eaten. We interviewed my former associate pastor who grew up in England. He gave us pointers on what sauce to use, how the dish started, and how each region offers the dish slightly differently. Next, we interviewed another colleague who grew up in Puerto Rico. He FaceTimed us the entire time we were making black beans, pork, and rice. He talked about his family and how his *abuela* would make the fried plantains just so. We had Mediterranean dishes, Egyptian desserts, and sushi, all the while hearing stories from old and new friends, and why these dishes were important to them. Breaking bread is more than just eating. It is communion with each other. It is a way to well remember the past.

Maybe this is why we have no record of Jesus eating alone. Food is a vehicle through which we connect with our history, our friends, and even our enemies. Over and over again we have stories of Jesus eating with people. He eats with sinners; he eats with saints. He was labeled a glutton and a drunkard. His disciples picked grain on the Sabbath. He fed thousands with almost nothing, identified himself as the bread from heaven, and took that same bread, broke it, gave it holy significance as his body, and offers it to us. From farm to table, no one truly eats alone, and I think that first Christmas taught us this all along.

When we gather around the Lord's Table, we remember and celebrate that Jesus offers his body as nourishment. Where did he get such an idea? Could it be that the grace and humility with which Mary offered her body to Jesus informed Jesus's understanding

Breaking bread is more than just eating. It is communion with each other. It is a way to well remember the past.

of his body as nourishment for us? Every Sunday when I serve Communion, I invite the community to come forward by saying, "Taste how good the Lord is." Tasting the Lord's goodness is not about flavor or Hawaiian bread or the brand of juice we use. It is the recognition that we are all hungry, we all need food to survive, and Jesus offers himself to us with reckless abandon.

QUESTIONS

1. What are your favorite Christmas dishes or desserts? Why do you think we eat so many foods that are unique to this time of year?

2. How do the dishes we eat at this time of year signify our anticipation and expectation for the coming Jesus?

3. Have you ever thought about Mary nursing baby Jesus, giving him his first meal? How does this highlight the vulnerability God takes on in the Incarnation?

4. Do you think Jesus had a favorite food? What does it say about God that Jesus lived in a particular time and place, including characteristic flavors, dishes, and experiences of food?

5. How does food bring us together with others? What opportunities do you have in your congregation and in your family or community to come together around food?

CHAPTER FOUR

DO YOU FEEL WHAT I FEEL?

CHAPTER FOUR

DO YOU FEEL WHAT I FEEL?

"Your savior is born today in David's city. He is Christ the Lord."

(Luke 2:11)

There are three things I mention at the end of a wedding rehearsal before dismissing everyone with prayer. First, I tell everyone to be sure to eat enough during the day. Your wedding attire is going to fit the way it's going to fit regardless of what you eat the day of the ceremony. A wedding day can be quite hectic, so you must fuel your body well. No one wants to see you pass out because you forgot to each lunch. Second, I remind them to drink enough water throughout the day, and I emphasize that water is what should be consumed. Sometimes people, and particularly groomsmen, forget that they are supposed to be preparing for a religious ceremony, not tailgating before a game.

The third thing I mention might sound silly, but if a wedding party gets it wrong, the congregation feels like something is off. They might not even be able to articulate why, but they will feel that something isn't quite right. This third thing is what to do with your hands. The women in the party typically are holding a bouquet. That's easy enough. The men in the party need some extra guidance. They shouldn't "do the butler" (with their hands behind their back) because we aren't shooting an episode of *Downton Abbey*. They also shouldn't do the "penalty kick" (holding their hands in front) because this isn't the World Cup. Neither should they put their hands in their pockets, which communicates that they would rather be somewhere else. That's not a good look. I instruct them simply to relax their hands and put them at their sides. It feels awkward, but it looks the most natural.

It's also important for the couple getting married to do the right things with their hands. During the ceremony, from the time they are brought together until after the end of the ceremony, they are never not touching. They are either arm in arm or hand in hand. I've learned over time and many weddings how important this is. It may seem to be a small thing, but seeing the couple not physically connected to each other doesn't feel right.

Our hands are often so busy. What is it that you do with your hands most often during the day? What occupies your hands the most? For example, does plastic occupy your hands most of the day because you're typing at a keyboard or playing video games? Is glass at your fingertips most often because of your smart phone? Unless you're a nurse, physical therapist, or personal trainer, I'm assuming what isn't at the top of your list is human touch. Yet human touch, physical contact with others, is an important part of our lives.

Tiffany Field, a researcher at the University of Miami School of Medicine noted in a *New York Times* article in 2017 that no one at her airport terminal was touching each other. That might seem common for strangers, but couples who seemed together were only embracing their phones. Ms. Field's research has concluded that good, physical touch leads to lower blood pressure, lower cases of anxiety, and higher life expectancy. In children there is less aggression, and fewer incidents of bullying. She studied an orphanage in Romania where the data suggested that lack of touch contributed to growth stunting. Healthy touch is a good thing. We seem to be hardwired physically to be with each other.

Tim Reiner, the author of the *New York Times* article begins the piece saying:

> I had thought about reaching for my father's hand for weeks. He was slowly dying in a nursing home, and no one who visited him — from my mother, his wife of 42 years, to my three siblings — held his hand. How do you reach for something that, for so many decades, hinted at violence and, worse, dismissal?

In the flickering gray from the old black-and-white movies we watched together, I finally did it. I touched my father's hand, which I hadn't held since I was a young boy. His curled fingers opened, unhinging some long-sealed door within me, then lightly closed around mine. Before I left, I did something else none of the males in my family had ever done before. I leaned close to my father's ear and whispered, "I love you."[1]

Do you see what I see? We can navigate the world without sight—it's difficult, but possible. Do you hear what I hear? Many people can live quite well without a sense of hearing. COVID-19 taught many of us that even though it's a drag, we can live without taste. We cannot live without touch. It would be impossible. We must be able to feel the world around us.

THE POWER OF TOUCH

My mother has these fantastic sayings. Remember, when I called home after eating a pound of raw chicken, my mother's response was, "Son, that's just natural selection trying to take you out of the gene pool." I remember when I was very young, she was in the kitchen and warned me that the stove was hot. I mean, what does she know, really? Of course I touched the stove and burned my hand. What did my mother say? "Well, it didn't take you long to look at that, did it?" Our sense of touch protects us. That protection might initially be painful, but coiling our hand after the sensation of intense heat on the fingertips prevents further damage. That feeling in the pit of your stomach when something doesn't feel quite right might end up saving you from a

We cannot live
without touch.
It would be
impossible.
We must be able
to feel the world
around us.

lot of trouble. Feeling the hair on the back of your neck stand up primes you to be ready for whatever might be lurking around the next corner. My son, Robert, started karate not long ago. It's been such a joy to see him discovering how to move his body, feeling where his body begins and ends, and learning touch responsibly to protect himself or someone else. Being intentional about how his body moves through space has caused him to be much more thoughtful and aware of those around him. Good, healthy touch protects.

Touch also helps communicate. When you're anxious, a hug from a trusted friend says, "Everything is going to be alright." A slap on the back or a high five just before the game can hype up a teammate and say, "Let's go!" An expectant mother doing kick counts in her third trimester helps make sure that all is well with the baby. As Tim Reiner shows, good healthy touch can say, "I love you." Touch can soothe and center, like rubbing your child's back when he or she feels sick or receiving a massage at the end of a stressful week.

Touch can protect and communicate, soothe and center. Touch is also complicated. Every time we gather for worship, we "pass the peace" just prior to Communion. After inviting the congregation to stand, I announce, "Christ invites to his table all who love him, who earnestly repent of their sin, and who seek to live in peace with one another; therefore let us show signs of peace among one another." Of course, this is an introvert's nightmare, and early in my tenure in my current church, it showed. The passing of the peace lasted less than a minute, with minimal movement and lots of silence. Over time the passing of the peace seems to get just a touch longer every week. Handshakes and hugs and lots of conversation and laughter seem to take more time as the weeks go by. That's not a bad thing, unless it is. Although passing the peace isn't mandatory, for those who wrestle with touch, especially the touch of people they don't know, this part of the worship experience can get tricky. No one wants to be perceived as rude, but so much movement can feel chaotic and unsettling for those with sensory issues. We all have personal bubbles, and some are larger than others. Touch needs permission. Touch is so powerful that, if used inappropriately, it can cause incredible harm that takes a lifetime to heal.

During Advent we prepare for the Incarnation. We prepare not only for God entering into time and creation, but for God assuming our humanity. God has eyes to see our suffering and celebrations. God has ears to hear our cheers and laments. For the first time, God eats and drinks to live. But the most profound of all the senses God assumes is the sense of touch. To know what it is like to be full and what it is like to be empty. The pleasure of that first morning stretch, the pain of a skinned knee, and the healing of a mother's embrace. This fully divine and fully human Jesus certainly had growing pains and experienced the confusion of puberty, the headaches of dehydration, and the joy of a friend's embrace.

Jesus also used the power of touch for healing. Luke 7 records:

> *A little later Jesus went to a city called Nain. His disciples and a great crowd traveled with him. As he approached the city gate, a dead man was being*

Most profound of all the senses God assumes is the sense of touch. To know what it is like to be full and what it is like to be empty. The pleasure of that first morning stretch, the pain of a skinned knee, and the healing of a mother's embrace.

carried out. He was his mother's only son, and she was a widow. A large crowd from the city was with her. When he saw her, the Lord had compassion for her and said, "Don't cry." He stepped forward and touched the stretcher on which the dead man was being carried. Those carrying him stood still. Jesus said, "Young man, I say to you, get up." The dead man sat up and began to speak, and Jesus gave him to his mother.

Awestruck, everyone praised God. "A great prophet has appeared among us," they said. "God has come to help his people." This news about Jesus spread throughout Judea and the surrounding region.

(Luke 7:11-17)

Interestingly the people's first reaction wasn't celebration or elation; rather it was a shocked stillness and then fear. Why? Jesus touched the funeral bier. Whether the shock was from a ritual uncleanliness or the interruption of a solemn procession, Jesus healed the man and raised him from the dead. You aren't supposed to be able to do that. Godly people are clean and orderly people...and Jesus challenges this over and over again. Later in the same chapter:

One of the Pharisees invited Jesus to eat with him. After he entered the Pharisee's home, he took his place at the table. Meanwhile, a woman from the city, a sinner, discovered that Jesus was dining in the Pharisee's house. She brought perfumed oil in a vase made of alabaster. Standing behind him at his feet and crying, she began to wet his feet with her tears. She wiped them with her hair, kissed them, and poured the oil on them. When the Pharisee who had invited Jesus saw what was happening, he said to himself, If this man were a prophet, he would know what kind of woman is touching him. He would know that she is a sinner.

Jesus replied, "Simon, I have something to say to you."

"Teacher, speak," he said.

"A certain lender had two debtors. One owed enough money to pay five hundred people for a day's work. The other owed enough money for fifty. When they couldn't pay, the lender forgave the debts of them both. Which of them will love him more?"

Simon replied, "I suppose the one who had the largest debt canceled."

Jesus said, "You have judged correctly."

Jesus turned to the woman and said to Simon, "Do you see this woman? When I entered your home, you didn't give me water for my feet, but she wet my feet with tears and wiped them with her hair. You didn't greet me with a kiss, but she hasn't stopped kissing my feet since I came in. You didn't anoint my head with oil, but she has poured perfumed oil on my feet. This is why I tell you that her many sins have been forgiven; so she has shown great love. The one who is forgiven little loves little."

Then Jesus said to her, "Your sins are forgiven."

*The other table guests began to say among themselves,
"Who is this person that even forgives sins?"*

*Jesus said to the woman, "Your faith has saved you.
Go in peace."*

(Luke 7:36-50)

Similarly in the next chapter, a woman who had been bleeding for twelve years touched the hem of his garment. Jesus asks, "Who touched me." Peter who is standing there says, "Don't you see this crowd around you? How can you say who touched you."

*But Jesus said, "Someone touched me. I know that
power has gone out from me."*

*When the woman saw that she couldn't escape notice,
she came trembling and fell before Jesus. In front of
everyone, she explained why she had touched him and
how she had been immediately healed.*

*"Daughter, your faith has healed you," Jesus said. "Go
in peace."*

(Luke 8:46-48)

In both stories someone reached out to Jesus, in both stories Jesus was made unclean according to the law, in both stories healing still happened, and in both stories Jesus says, "Your faith has healed you." Faith in what? I've heard it preached that if you are faithful enough and believe in Jesus enough, then things like illness, poverty, failures...won't happen. Conversely we have the idea that if you have money in the bank, are in good health, and your spouse is attractive, then you must be really faithful and you have been blessed. You and I both know that this is a lie told by people who want the world to think they have it all together.

"Your faith has made you well/saved you." Faith in what, exactly? It's faith in Jesus—faith that Jesus would not turn them away. Faith that Jesus would not shun them or send them out. Faith that Jesus would offer divine compassion. Faith that what they had been told about themselves was not the truth. Faith that God in the flesh was the source of their restoration. Jesus did not recoil from their touch, and neither would God. That moment of acceptance was the beginning of a journey of healing.

In Luke's Gospel there seems to be a current of good, healthy touching that has profound bookends. At the beginning of Jesus's story, Simeon takes Jesus into his arms, into a full embrace. This certainly wasn't the only time Jesus was held as an infant, but even in his birth narrative it says that Jesus was placed in a manger, so Luke is making a point here.

> Simeon took Jesus in his arms and praised God. He said,
>
>> "Now, master, let your servant go in peace according to your word,
>>> because my eyes have seen your salvation.
>> You prepared this salvation in the presence of all peoples.
>> It's a light for revelation to the Gentiles
>>> and a glory for your people Israel."
>>>> (Luke 2:28-32)

It says that Simeon was righteous and devout and was awaiting the kingdom of God. His full embrace of Jesus announced that salvation was for all, full of revelation and glory. What is that salvation? Turn to the end of the story.

> *Now there was a man named Joseph who was a member of the council. He was a good and righteous man. He hadn't agreed with the plan and actions of the council. He was from the Jewish city of Arimathea and eagerly anticipated God's kingdom. This man went to Pilate and asked for Jesus' body. Taking it down, he wrapped it in a linen cloth and laid it in a tomb carved out of the rock, in which no one had ever been buried.*
> *(Luke 23:50-53)*

These were the only two times that the Gospels recall Jesus's body being fully embraced. Through Luke's Gospel we see that through touch, the sense we cannot live without, we see the revelation and glory that God will stop at nothing to bring us in, messy and screwed up as we are, into a godly embrace for healing and wholeness, community and communion. There's a lesson hidden in the touches offered to Jesus. He was fully embraced at his infancy. He was fully embraced at his death. Luke seems to communicate that to fully embrace Christ, we are to take hold of the entire story.

John's Gospel gives us an even fuller picture of the complexity of touch. The Resurrection account in John's Gospel reminds us that good touch is not always about holding on. Sometimes it means knowing when to let go. When Mary recognizes the risen Christ on that first Easter Sunday morning, he says to her, "Don't hold on to me, for I haven't yet gone up to my Father… to my God and your God" (John 20:17). Lots of scholars have tried

There's a lesson hidden in the touches offered to Jesus. He was fully embraced at his infancy. He was fully embraced at his death. Luke seems to communicate that to fully embrace Christ, we are to take hold of the entire story.

to make sense of this strange prohibition. Is Jesus commanding a physical distance between him and Mary? Maybe Jesus is talking about lingering or holding on to a relationship that will now be forever changed. It seems too simple to assume that this interaction is a metaphor for trying a new worship style or living into a pastoral change. At least, it would be a bold choice to read this at my retirement-from-ministry party, assuming that folks aren't holding the door open and shoving me out the door!

I'm not quite sure of the original intent, but I have officiated plenty of funerals where holding our memories loosely is the beginning of the healing of grief. We know that Mary was weeping, and that weeping will continue if she doesn't say goodbye well. Jesus is clear that he is leaving and that Mary has a job to do. "Go to my brothers and sisters and tell them, 'I'm going up to my Father and your Father, to my God and your God'" (John 20:17b). We aren't offered any detail as to what Jesus means, except that this Ascension is an invitation into the heart of God. Jesus incorporates the disciples into this dramatic event saying, "My God and your God." Saying goodbye well means recognizing that our story is larger than ourselves. When we invite our loved ones into the arms of God, we know one day the same liturgy will be read for us, and there will be no room for these pesky perceived dividing lines between us when we are with "My God and your God." Letting go, holding loosely to what was, doesn't dishonor the past or dismiss the story that makes us who we are, but it does allow us to live into the reality of the much bigger story that God has in mind. Recognizing this bigger picture may be why Mary says to the disciples, "I've seen the Lord" (John 20:18). Jesus is no longer "Rabbouni," or "Good Shepherd," or the vine that holds us together. Jesus is Lord. Maybe holding these other titles loosely is how we get to this amazing confession of faith.

Touch protects. Touch communicates. Touch soothes, centers, and heals—and it's complicated. I think the best way to think about the miracle of good, healthy touch is from a song by Mindy Smith, which echoes the story of Tim Reiner holding the hand of his father. Mindy Smith's song "One Moment More"[2] is a song she wrote for her mother when her mother was dying. She sings about wanting just another moment to hold her mother before she passes away, but it is enough to know that her mother isn't going far. So she sings softly, peacefully, and with a quiet strength in her voice. The last line, sung with little accompaniment and a hushed voice of goodbye, lingers longer than you might expect when you hear, "Hold me, even though I know you're leaving." The music rings on the dominant chord of the key, not moving to the root or "home" of the key, suggesting that the song isn't quite over, but it fades out anyway. In other words, the song is over, but the story isn't.

A SENSE-ABLE GOD

Christmas looks different. We put lights on our homes and decorations in our windows. We adorn our towns with red and green and gold. Our streets (and sometimes even our cars) show us that Christmas is coming. Even our behavior changes. We see more people serving others, celebrating in restaurants, visiting neighbors. *Things just look different this time of year because all of creation, with intent or accident, recognizes that when God put on flesh, everything changed.* We look at the world and ask God, "Do you see what I see? Do you see the hungry? Do you see the poor? Do you see those who are put down, messed up, ignored, or forgotten?" Now for the first time, because God has eyes to see, God answers by asking us the same questions. "Do you see what *I* see? Do you see that soon the hungry will be filled, the poor will be blessed, the persecuted will leap for joy? *I will walk among you, I will call you to follow, and together we will change the world.*"

God not only saw, but God heard. God spoke with Adam and Eve in the garden, God heard Abel's blood crying out of the ground, God heard the desperation of Hagar in the wilderness, God heard the begging and pleading and the suffering when God's people were enslaved in Egypt. God's ears were tuned to the cries of humanity. At Christmas our ears are tuned to hear songs of joy and jingling bells and winter wonderlands. From Wham! to Nat King Cole, everything we hear seems different this time of year, and it is because *all of creation, with intent or accident, recognizes that when God put on flesh, everything changed.* We call out to God, "Do you hear what I hear? Do you hear caroling and laughter and melodies that celebrate your coming into the world?" Now that God has ears in the person of Jesus, God will reply by asking us the same question. "Do you hear what *I* hear?" I hear the joy and the Merry Christmas in the market, and I also hear your laments and the silent sniffling of those who hold sorrow in secret. I hear

All of creation,
with intent
or accident,
recognizes that
when God put on
flesh, everything
changed.

the prayers of a child putting peace and security on her Christmas list. Hear me when I say:

> *Comfort, comfort my people!*
> *says your God.*
> *Speak compassionately to Jerusalem,*
>   *and proclaim to her that her compulsory*
> *service has ended,*
>   *that her penalty has been paid,*
> *that she has received from the LORD's hand*
>   *double for all her sins!*
>   *(Isaiah 40:1-2)*

Soon you will hear words that call for loving your enemy, words of healing for those who are sick; you will hear that if we are told to be quiet that the rocks and stones themselves will sing out. *I will walk among you, I will call you to follow, and together we will change the world.*

Not only in the person of Jesus does God see with divine eyes and hear with holy ears, but God will for the first time know hunger and thirst. Let us not forget that on the first Christmas, Mary, the nursing Madonna, offered her body to sustain the body of the One who sustains us with his through bread and wine, body broken and blood outpoured. Could it be that the humility, intimacy, and holiness of nursing is why Jesus saw the significance of his last supper? Jesus understood there is no greater connection with each other and the divine than when we gather around the table to remember Jesus saying that this is *my* body offered for you. Every time you eat. Every time you feed. Every time you prepare the table for family, friend, and enemy, be mindful of me.

Feeling the hunger pains in the wilderness may be why Jesus so often sat around the table with saint and sinner alike.

Not only are the sights and sounds different this time of year, but how we set the table has changed. Gingerbread and cranberries and sugar cookies and figgy pudding adorn the table. Even what we eat is different this time of year because *all of creation, with intent or accident, recognizes that when God put on flesh, everything changed.* We ask, "Do you taste what I taste? Do you taste the sweetness of sugarplums and cookies left at the fireplace?" Now that God in the flesh knows what it means to be sustained with food and drink, God will reply by asking us the same question. "Do you taste what *I* taste? Yes, I love the winter harvest. But I am also mindful of those who hungered as I did, and those who know the exhaustion of dehydration. I want my people to taste and see how good the Lord is. *I will walk among you, I will call you to follow, and together we will change the world.*"

Sights, sounds, hunger, and also touch. God will know what it means to embrace and what it means to be held, to know the power and responsibility of touch, the confusion of puberty, and also the pain of crucifixion. Hands that reached out for his mother will be hands outstretched revealing the vulnerable and passionate love God has for all of creation. Even touch seems different this time of year—the embrace of family who've been away for far too long, the choosing and wrapping of packages for excited friends, waxy fingers holding a tiny candle during "Silent Night." Everything feels different this time of year because *all of creation, with intent or accident, recognizes that when God put on flesh, everything changed.* We ask, "Do you feel what I feel? Do you

116

feel the chill in the air? Do you feel the sharpness of the evergreen decorating the chancel"? Now for the first time God will reply by asking us the same question. "Do you feel what *I* feel? I feel the warmth of a coat given to a stranger, the soothing of pain from reconciled enemies, and the joy and excitement of gifts given to those who thought their stockings would be bare. *I will walk among you, I will call you to follow, and together we will change the world.*"

IN THOSE DAYS...ON THIS DAY...YOU WILL SEE

Experiencing Christmas began with "In those days." "In those days" offers a picture of what was. Caesar ordered the world, the powerful made the rules, and only the elite mattered. It is a miracle that we know anything about Jesus. A child born to a family in poverty in an occupied land would not be important enough to remember. Luke's call to "those days" reminds us of the contrast between God and Caesar. In both the Creation story and this inbreaking of a new creation with God-in-the-flesh, we have those with power speaking a decree to the ends of the earth. Both God and Caesar have a desire to order the world. God subdues the darkness with light, the waters with land, the empty sky with celestial bodies until we find a relative pause when humanity is born. There is a definitive rhythm with Caesar's proclamation as well. From the palace to Quirinius, then Joseph to Mary, and finally the birth of the Second Adam as Paul alludes in Romans. Both stories have a rhythm and direction, but in the beginning

God is building in order for creation and creator to rest in one another in mutual and shared adoration. Luke presents an earthly descent of importance so that the Pax Romana, the Roman Peace, might spread through the land in terror and fear. Caesar wants all to be counted, not to measure their worth, but to calculate their value to the empire. With Caesar there is no Sabbath. There is no time for rest when you constantly must look over your shoulder for potential successors. When Christ is born, the world of "In those days" is turned on its head.

In those days Caesar had the power to order and move the world, but God is doing something new. An angel, a heavenly messenger, appeared not in the palace or to Caesar, or any member of the court, but the divine presence was revealed to the shepherds. God seems to be doing this all wrong. If God really wants to get noticed, the angels would have appeared to Caesar, but "In those days" is soon to be over.

The beginning of Luke's Nativity is proclaimed in past tense. "In those days" *was* the first registration. Joseph *went* to Bethlehem because he was a descendant of David. Joseph *was* engaged to Mary, she *was* expecting a child, and there *was* no room for them in the guestroom. The entire saga from the palace to the manger is written in the past tense. This might not seem important until the heavens open up and the angels appear saying, "Don't be afraid! Look! I bring good news to you—wonderful, joyous news for all people. Your savior is born today in David's city. He is Christ the Lord" (Luke 2:10-11).

The angel's words are in the present. The proclamation from heaven signals that "In those days" are over. The present proclamation is poignant because it speaks to the miracle of the Incarnation. The present is the only portion of time that feels real to us. The past is a memory and the future is a dream, but the present is real as far as real can be. When God puts on flesh in the person of Jesus, God adopts our senses. Not only does God have eyes to see and ears to hear, but now time becomes relevant in the life of the divine. We cannot see into the future just as we cannot see what is behind us. Sounds crescendo and fade and must be remembered. Our spirit may never hunger and thirst again, but our bodies need constant sustenance. We cannot touch the past, which is why loving embraces linger.

The angel continues and offers the shepherds a future trajectory—"This is a sign for you: you will find a newborn baby wrapped snugly and lying in a manger" (Luke 2:12). It is definitive. There is no room for maybe in this new, inbreaking creation. Christmas Eve is a silent night because Christmas is the eye of the hurricane, a wind burdened with passion and fervor and faith and justice and a peace that surpasses all understanding so that "In those days" gives way for "Today," so that all our days will know the salvation offered through Jesus's defeat of death. In those days God did see and hear, but today heaven and earth collide so that we will never see and hear and taste and touch the same ever again. In those days a decree went out from Emperor Augustus that all the world should be counted, but today your savior is born in David's city, a savior who is Christ the Lord. Today everything is changed. Just like a child's cry with eyes closed remembers God's first words before the light of sight, may the night we celebrate Christ's birth be a beginning that remembers the beginning so that all of our senses will be devoted to the new creation born from Jesus who lived, who died, and who rose again so that Creator and creation might be one.

GOD IS WITH US

Experiencing Christmas is not just about knowing that God shares in the faulty senses we use to navigate our every day in order to redeem our every day. Throughout this study there is a trajectory that brings us into communion with Christ in a way that you might not realize. We begin with sight, because maybe the things we see are the most obvious signs that Christmas is coming. Long before the carols are sung or the traditional dishes are served, department stores and television commercials try to grab our attention with reds and greens and stars and trees. In a way, we can "see" Christmas coming long before it arrives, when the calendar is barely into November. Of all our senses, sight allows us the most distance. For years when my family would go on vacation, we would take the coast road along the Gulf of Mexico from Louisiana to Florida. If the weather was clear, my dad would always point out that you could see individual trees on Cat Island, a barrier island off the Mississippi Gulf coast. It became an inside joke every time we made the turn to follow the coast. As soon as we left the interstate for the highway, we'd hear, "Did you know on a clear day you can see individual trees on Cat Island?"

Sight allows for distance. I can see you long before I can hear you. We can see airplanes flying overhead and mountains in the distance. We can see the sun, moon, and stars. With amazing new technology, we can see the light all the way back to the first stars of the universe. In this way, sight and hope go together. Hope offers the biggest picture for the future. Hope transforms our Advent anticipation into a holy expectation of God's inbreaking miracle. Lighting the candle of hope on the first Sunday of Advent sets a beautiful tone for the story that is soon to unfold. The light of hope can be far away, but when our vision matches the will of God, there is no darkness or distance that can overcome it.

On a clear day I may be able to see the individual trees on Cat Island, but I can't hear you from quite that far away. Listening to you, hearing what you have to say, and having a conversation means I need to be a bit closer to you. Of course there are exceptions—sound travels farther in water, and technology allows us to talk by phone from across the planet—but hearing normally requires nearness. To be in someone's presence without aid and share words with each other necessitates more intimacy than the distance sight affords. Formal declarations can be broadcast to thousands, but with the kind of conversation you don't want everyone to hear, you have to be close.

In this way, our sense of sound and the candle of peace go together. We must be close if there is to be peace. Peace is the fruition of forgiveness, compromise, and reconciliation. Our ideas and desire must be more closely aligned for war to be a memory. I remember several years ago we had to let a staff member go. It was painful and ugly, and my least favorite thing about ministry. Even though letting him go was the right thing to do, I didn't blame his family for being upset. He still worshipped with us every Sunday, but during the passing of the peace he stood still with his arms crossed, which was a sure sign that I was not welcome to come any closer than the distance between the pulpit and his pew. One Sunday I noticed his arms weren't crossed, so I took my chance. As I walked toward him his arms began to fold, but just before they did, I reached out my hand. He took it. We locked eyes with an expression that said, "We're OK," and we've been shaking hands ever since. Whether the distance between us is real or realized, we must be close to hear the sound of peace.

The sound of peace calls us to be closer to one another than does the light of hope, but to break bread with one another, for you to taste the same thing I'm tasting, means we have to be at the same table. It is not an exaggeration to say that food is made with love. Eating with another person is an intimate act. Making room for each other at the table takes vulnerability. Sharing the same dish takes planning and care. This is part of the beauty of Holy Communion. The more you gather at the same table with your neighbor, the more you share the same loaf of bread and same cup of juice, the more the Holy Spirit transforms you to recognize that we aren't nearly as different as we might pretend to be. Although our tastes are unique, and can drive our passions in wildly different directions, breaking bread together always reminds us that we all need to eat, and we should all be able to. Hope can be seen at a distance. Even a whisper can carry when the acoustics are right. If you and I are breaking bread, you cannot be farther than arm's length away. Sitting at the same table offers us a taste of the kind of love Jesus promises when, by the end of the story, we feast at the heavenly banquet.

Jesus is fully human
and fully divine,
without division,
embodied with a sense
of touch that will
know what it means
to be held, to be cared
for, and also to know
pain and sorrow.

The light of hope, the sound of peace, a taste of love, and finally a touch of joy. Joy is the steadfast assurance that God is with us. Finally, the distance between us and the divine becomes indistinguishable. Jesus is fully human and fully divine, without division, embodied with a sense of touch that will know what it means to be held, to be cared for, and also to know pain and sorrow. Touch is not only about what our hands can hold or how we are held, but all that accompanies our emotions. In Jesus, God knows happiness and loss, excitement and curiosity. More than once Jesus told the disciples not to worry and to have no fear, because I'm sure a time or two he felt the potential of how difficult anxiety could be. Jesus told parables about rejoicing and celebrating, knowing what it feels like for the heart to race when a lost sheep is found. Joy is the touch of the divine for which our Advent expectation has been building. With each passing week of preparation, the divine comes increasingly closer to us until God becomes one of us. God enters creation in a forever-present presence so that we might see hope, hear peace, taste love, and feel joy. May we share in God's vision that all shall be saved. May we share in the singing of the heavenly host. May we taste the love set around the Communion table. May it all come together with a touch of joy with the ever-present reality that to us is born a Savior!

QUESTIONS

1. Think about your typical day and week. What things do you touch most often? How often do you experience human touch?

2. What sorts of touch did Jesus experience, both as a baby and as an adult?

3. Human touch is powerful. How did Jesus use touch to heal? How might you offer healing touch to those around you?

4. In Jesus, God took on a human body and experienced all of our human senses. What does this say about God? What does it say about human life and the kind of relationship we can have with God?

5. How has your experience of Advent this year been different? How have the sights, sounds, tastes, and other senses signified to you the coming of Jesus, God with us?

AFTERWORD

A PLEASING AROMA

I know what you're thinking. How could you talk about the senses of the season and not talk about smell? When I offered this worship series in my congregation, I jokingly began my Christmas Eve sermon talking about what the first Christmas must have smelled like. I could sense how uneasy the congregation was as I started to describe Jesus being born among the cattle, donkeys, and whoever else couldn't fit in the stable guest room. To their relief, I changed direction in my sermon, but it was fun to see them squirm for a moment.

Smell is certainly an important sense, especially with its connection with memory. On the first Sunday of Advent, I go from pew to pew spraying an evergreen scent in the sanctuary before the service begins. I want even the smell of the room to mark the difference of the season. The smell of the Christmas tree marks the season for me. When you think of Christmas, you may be mindful of the smell of your grandmother's house, sugar cookies, or gingerbread in the oven. Or maybe it's the industrial smell of tape and wrapping paper that signals the season for you. When I smell a Christmas tree, I can't help but feel the excitement of Christmas.

Smell revealed an important truth to me this past year. One day my wife, Christie, got a new perfume, and it wasn't my favorite scent. In fact, it was noxious. For two and a half months I played in my head how I was going to mention that the perfume was really bothering me. I finally drummed up the courage to say something to her as we were leaving our children's elementary school program. "Your perfume is really strong," I said. "I can smell it all day." Christie replied, "No you can't. It's eau de toilette. It evaporates quickly. I can barely smell it now and I've just put it on."

I spoke my piece; she wasn't happy, but I moved on. Later in the evening around 9:00, she asked me about our conversation earlier. I mentioned that I could still smell the perfume even though it had been hours since she put it on and she was at least seven feet away from me. So we played a game. I closed my eyes and she walked past me, and every time I was able to tell where she was. Frustrated, we asked Annaleigh her opinion. She mentioned that she couldn't smell it at all. Bewildered, I invited Christie to go upstairs to my oldest daughter's room. We asked Isabelle her

2121211

opinion about the perfume and she nearly gagged, the scent was so strong. I felt affirmed, but there were still two more children to interview. We went to my two youngest children's room. One of them could smell it and the other couldn't. Fascinating! We were all right in our own way.

Everyone agreed that Christie had put perfume on that day. That seems a silly thing to ask, but our interaction with the perfume was wildly different. It's like how some people appreciate cilantro, but others find it tastes like soap. For whatever reason, half of us just could not appreciate the scent. This is an important reminder that truth is objective, but our experience of it never is. Everything we know or experience is filtered through our senses, and our senses can lie to us. It's important to remember that my experience is not synonymous with my neighbor's experience. When we talk about worship, music, decorations, language, you name it, we can all have quite a different preference, experience, or reaction to what we might assume is common. It's not that truth is subjective, or I am the locus of truth without any outside confirmation or help, but my experience might not be the same as yours, and that has to be OK.

No single person owns the monopoly on experience or truth. The more we lean into this understanding, I think the easier it is to love and serve our neighbor. Paul writes,

> But thank God, who is always leading us around through Christ as if we were in a parade. He releases the fragrance of the knowledge of him everywhere through us. We smell like the aroma of Christ's offering to God, both to those who are being saved and to those

who are on the road to destruction. We smell like a contagious dead person to those who are dying, but we smell like the fountain of life to those who are being saved.

"Who is qualified for this kind of ministry?
(2 Corinthians 2:14-16)

May we be the "aroma of Christ's offering to God." What do you suppose that aroma may be? I'm sure it smells a lot like "love, joy, peace, patience, kindness, goodness, faithfulness, gentleness, and self-control" (Galatians 5:22-23). There is no [stench] against such things. May you have eyes to see the Good News. May your ears ring with praise and thanksgiving. May you taste the goodness of God. May you embrace your neighbor with great love. And may you be the aroma of Christ's offering to God in all that you do this Advent and Christmas season!